Madam President: The First Term of Kamala Harris

Vivian Ellis

Published by Kokosnuss Press, 2024.

While every precaution has been taken in the preparation of this book, the publisher assumes no responsibility for errors or omissions, or for damages resulting from the use of the information contained herein.

MADAM PRESIDENT: THE FIRST TERM OF KAMALA HARRIS

First edition. August 12, 2024.

Copyright © 2024 Vivian Ellis.

ISBN: 979-8227434579

Written by Vivian Ellis.

Table of Contents

Not like the brazen giant of Greek fame,

With conquering limbs astride from land to land;

Here at our sea-washed, sunset gates shall stand

A mighty woman with a torch, whose flame

Is the imprisoned lightning, and her name

Mother of Exiles. From her beacon-hand

Glows world-wide welcome; her mild eyes
command

The air-bridged harbor that twin cities frame.

"Keep, ancient lands, your storied pomp!" cries she

With silent lips. "Give me your tired, your poor,

Your huddled masses yearning to breathe free,

The wretched refuse of your teeming shore.

Send these, the homeless, tempest-tost to me,

I lift my lamp beside the golden door!"

Emma Lazarus, 1883

Introduction: A Presidency of Firsts and Lasting Change

THE STORY OF KAMALA Harris's presidency is one of historic firsts, transformative leadership, and a profound commitment to the ideals of justice, equality, and progress. As the first woman, the first Black woman, and the first person of South Asian descent to hold the office of President of the United States, Harris shattered barriers and redefined what was possible in American politics. Her ascent to the highest office in the land was not just a personal achievement, but a milestone in the nation's ongoing journey toward a more inclusive and representative democracy.

This book chronicles the pivotal moments, challenges, and triumphs of Kamala Harris's presidency, offering a detailed exploration of her impact on the United States and the world. It is a story of resilience in the face of unprecedented crises—a global economic downturn, a lingering pandemic, and deep political polarization. It is also a story of hope and renewal, as Harris led the nation through a period of significant transformation, advancing bold policies that sought to create a more just and equitable society.

Throughout her presidency, Harris demonstrated a unique blend of empathy and pragmatism, qualities that defined her leadership style and endeared her to millions of Americans. From her decisive actions on economic recovery and healthcare reform to her unwavering commitment to combating climate change and advancing civil rights, Harris's administration was marked by a determination to address the most pressing challenges of our time with both vision and resolve.

But Harris's presidency was about more than just policy. It was about representation—about showing the world that the highest office in the land was not just for a select few, but for anyone, regardless of gender, race, or background. Her partnerships with Vice President Tim Walz, and later Vice President Alexandria Ocasio-Cortez, another trailblazing leader, further underscored this message, signaling a new era of leadership that was diverse, dynamic, and deeply connected to the lived experiences of ordinary Americans.

This book dives into the key moments that defined Harris's time in office, from her historic inauguration to her successful re-election campaign, and the legacy she left behind. It explores the long-term effects of her policies on American society and the global stage, as well as the challenges she faced in a deeply divided political landscape.

Kamala Harris's presidency was not just a chapter in the history of the United States; it was a turning point—a moment when the nation took bold steps toward a more inclusive, just, and prosperous future. This is the story of that journey.

Chapter 1: Inauguration Day

The Historic Moment: January 20, 2025

The brisk winter air of Washington, D.C. held a special kind of electricity on January 20, 2025. As the sun rose over the Capitol, its rays reflected off the white marble and gilded domes, signaling not just a new day, but a new era. It was a momentous occasion that the country and the world would long remember—a day when history would be made, not by the might of an army or the stroke of a legislative pen, but by the peaceful transfer of power, an enduring symbol of democracy. The anticipation had been building for months, and now, the world watched as Kamala Devi Harris prepared to take the oath of office as the 47th President of the United States.

Kamala Harris's path to this moment was unlike any other in American history. Born to a Jamaican father and an Indian mother, she had navigated a career that saw her break barriers at every turn—from becoming the first female District Attorney of San Francisco, to the first Black and South Asian woman elected Attorney General of California, and then as a U.S. Senator. Her tenure as Vice President under President Joe Biden had further solidified her position as a trailblazer. Now, standing on the cusp of becoming the nation's leader, she was poised to shatter the highest glass ceiling, not just for women, but for all underrepresented communities.

The morning of Inauguration Day was marked by a quiet resolve in Kamala. The weight of history pressed upon her, not as a burden, but as a mantle she had prepared to carry. Her thoughts were with her mother, Shyamala Gopalan Harris, who had passed away in 2009 but whose influence was etched into every fiber of Kamala's being. It was her mother's teachings on justice, equality, and service that had guided Kamala to this historic threshold. As she dressed in a purple coat—chosen to symbolize unity and the coming together of a divided nation—she took a moment to reflect on the journey that had led her to this day.

The crowd that gathered on the National Mall, though smaller in size due to lingering public health concerns, was no less enthusiastic. Supporters from all walks of life braved the cold, bundled in coats and scarves, some holding signs, others wrapped in blankets emblazoned with the stars and stripes. Their cheers echoed through the streets as the clock ticked closer to noon. The mood was one of celebration, optimism, and hope—a stark contrast to the darker days of the recent past.

The world watched, transfixed. Millions tuned in from every corner of the globe, recognizing that what was about to transpire would not only shape the future of the United States but would send ripples across the international stage. In homes, cafes, and public squares, people gathered around televisions and streamed the event on their devices, eager to witness history.

The Swearing-In Ceremony

At precisely noon, Chief Justice John Roberts stood before the assembled crowd on the West Front of the Capitol, holding the Bible that would serve as the conduit for the oath of office. Kamala Harris, her demeanor composed yet radiating confidence, approached the podium. The Bible she chose for the occasion had special significance—it was the one that belonged to Thurgood Marshall, the first Black Supreme Court Justice, a figure who had inspired her own legal career. The weight of its history was fitting for the occasion, linking the past struggles for civil rights with the present moment of triumph.

The moment was surreal, almost dreamlike. As Harris raised her right hand, placing her left on the Bible, the murmur of the crowd fell silent, replaced by the quiet hum of anticipation. The entire nation seemed to hold its breath.

"I, Kamala Devi Harris, do solemnly swear," she began, her voice clear and steady, "that I will faithfully execute the Office of President of the United States, and will to the best of my ability, preserve, protect, and defend the Constitution of the United States, so help me God."

With those words, Kamala Harris became the 47th President of the United States.

The crowd erupted into applause, a thunderous sound that reverberated across the Mall and through the streets of Washington. Tears streamed down the faces of many in the audience—tears of joy, of relief, of pride. It was a cathartic moment for a nation that had endured years of turmoil, division, and uncertainty. It was a moment that signaled not just the inauguration of a new president, but the dawning of a new chapter in American history.

The Role of Tim Walz

Just moments before Kamala Harris took her oath, Tim Walz had been sworn in as the Vice President of the United States. A seasoned politician with deep roots in Midwestern values, Walz was a steadying force in the administration, bringing with him years of experience as a Congressman and as the Governor of Minnesota. His pragmatic approach to governance, his dedication to the working class, and his military background made him an ideal partner for Harris in leading a diverse and often divided nation.

Walz's inauguration, though quieter than Harris's, was no less significant. It marked the continuation of a partnership that had been carefully cultivated during the campaign and would now be tested in the highest echelons of power. As he stood on the dais, flanked by his family, Walz took his oath with humility and a deep sense of responsibility.

The dynamic between Harris and Walz had been one of mutual respect and collaboration from the start. While Harris was the face of bold progressivism, Walz provided a grounded balance, appealing to the moderate and independent voters who had been crucial in securing the administration's victory. Together, they represented a coalition of values and ideals that aimed to heal the fractures within the country.

For Walz, the role of Vice President was one of action and influence. Unlike some of his predecessors who had occupied the office as mere figureheads, Walz was determined to be an active participant in the administration's efforts to govern. He was expected to take a lead role in working with Congress, particularly in building bridges with rural America, and to be a key advisor to Harris on both domestic and international issues. His reputation for bipartisanship and his ability to communicate across party lines would prove invaluable as the administration faced the formidable task of governing a polarized nation.

Reflections on the Significance

The significance of Kamala Harris's inauguration was not lost on those who witnessed it, both in person and through screens around the world. For many, it was the culmination of decades, even centuries, of struggle for equality and justice. It was a moment that echoed the dreams of suffragettes, civil rights activists, and every woman who had ever been told she couldn't. For Black Americans, for South Asians, for women, and for immigrants, Harris's ascension to the presidency was a powerful affirmation of the American ideal—that in this country, with hard work and perseverance, anything was possible.

The symbolism of the moment was profound. Harris's very presence at the pinnacle of power challenged the traditional narrative of American leadership. She represented a break from the past, a turning point where the voices that had long been marginalized were now at the forefront of national and global discourse. Her presidency was not just a victory for her or her supporters; it was a victory for democracy itself—a testament to its resilience and its capacity to evolve.

Internationally, Harris's presidency was seen as a beacon of hope and progress. In many parts of the world, particularly in countries where women and minorities still faced significant barriers, her rise to power was a source of inspiration. Leaders across the globe extended their congratulations, but also looked to Harris with expectations of renewed leadership on issues such as climate change, human rights, and global security. Her inauguration was more than an American milestone; it was a signal to the world that the U.S. was ready to re-engage on the global stage with a leader who embodied the principles of inclusion and diversity.

Yet, alongside the celebrations and the sense of historic achievement, there was also a sobering recognition of the challenges ahead. The country Harris inherited was one still deeply divided, with wounds that would not heal overnight. The economic disparities exacerbated by the pandemic, the ongoing racial tensions, the polarized political climate, and the looming threats of climate change and global instability—all these were daunting challenges that would require not just vision, but pragmatism, cooperation, and a relentless commitment to service.

Harris herself was acutely aware of these challenges. In her inaugural address, she struck a tone of determination and unity. She acknowledged the divisions within the country but emphasized that what united Americans was far greater than what divided them. She called for a new era of cooperation and civility, urging the nation to move forward together.

"Our diversity is our strength," she declared, her voice carrying across the Mall. "And it is our duty to ensure that every American, regardless of race, religion, gender, or background, has a seat at the table. We must reject the forces of hatred, intolerance, and division, and instead embrace the values of inclusion, respect, and empathy."

Her words were met with resounding applause, a hopeful note that echoed the sentiments of those who believed in the promise of a better future. But for Harris, the work was just beginning. She knew that her presidency would be judged not just by the history made on this day, but by the progress achieved in the years to come. The road ahead was long, and the challenges were many, but Kamala Harris was ready—ready to lead, ready to serve, and ready to make history.

The Inaugural Address

As Kamala Harris stood before the nation, having just taken the oath of office, she prepared to deliver her inaugural address—a speech that would set the tone for her presidency and outline the vision she had for the country. The address had been meticulously crafted, reflecting the input of her closest advisors, but also her own convictions and experiences. It was a speech designed not just to inspire, but to reassure a nation still reeling from the tumultuous years that had preceded it.

Harris's address was both a call to action and a promise of leadership. She pledged to govern with transparency, to seek out diverse perspectives, and to always put the needs of the American people first. She did not shy away from the challenges ahead, but instead embraced them as opportunities for growth and progress.

The address was met with widespread praise, even from some of her political opponents who recognized the sincerity of her message. It was a speech that resonated not just because of its content, but because of the person delivering it—a woman who had overcome countless obstacles to stand where she did, and who now carried the hopes and aspirations of millions on her shoulders.

The Global Reaction

As Kamala Harris concluded her inaugural address, the international response was immediate and overwhelmingly positive. World leaders from across the political spectrum offered their congratulations, many expressing optimism about the future of U.S. relations under her leadership.

MADAM PRESIDENT: THE FIRST TERM OF KAMALA HARRIS

In Europe, Harris's inauguration was seen as a return to stability and a recommitment to the transatlantic alliance. Leaders in Germany, France, and the United Kingdom spoke of their eagerness to work with the new administration on shared challenges such as climate change, trade, and security. For many in Europe, Harris's presidency was a welcome departure from the unpredictability of the previous administration, and a sign that the U.S. was ready to re-engage as a global leader.

In Asia, Harris's heritage was particularly celebrated. In India, the land of her maternal ancestors, there were jubilant scenes as people took to the streets to celebrate her achievement. Indian Prime Minister Narendra Modi was among the first to congratulate her, highlighting the deepening ties between the two nations. In Southeast Asia, Harris's presidency was seen as a positive development for U.S. relations with the region, particularly in terms of economic and security cooperation.

African nations, too, viewed Harris's inauguration with hope. Her heritage as the daughter of a Jamaican immigrant resonated deeply across the continent, where many saw her as a symbol of the African diaspora's potential. Several African leaders expressed their desire to strengthen ties with the U.S. and to work with Harris on issues such as development, trade, and climate change.

Even in regions where U.S. relations had been strained, there was a cautious optimism. In the Middle East, where conflicts and diplomatic tensions had long dominated U.S. policy,

Harris's presidency was seen as an opportunity for a fresh approach. While challenges remained, particularly with nations like Iran and Syria, there was a sense that Harris would bring a more diplomatic and measured tone to U.S. foreign policy.

In Latin America, leaders welcomed the possibility of more cooperative and respectful relations. Harris's focus on addressing the root causes of migration, improving economic conditions, and upholding human rights was seen as a positive shift from previous policies that had often been characterized by tension and conflict.

The global reaction to Harris's inauguration was a testament to the profound impact her presidency was expected to have not just in the United States, but around the world. It was a recognition that the values she embodied—diversity, justice, and equality—were not just American ideals, but universal ones.

A New Dawn

As the ceremonies of Inauguration Day drew to a close, the sense of a new beginning was palpable. The challenges that lay ahead were daunting, and the road to recovery and progress would be long. But there was also a renewed sense of hope—hope that the country could heal its divisions, that it could overcome the crises it faced, and that it could once again stand as a beacon of democracy and opportunity for the world.

MADAM PRESIDENT: THE FIRST TERM OF KAMALA HARRIS

Kamala Harris's journey to the presidency had been marked by perseverance, resilience, and an unwavering commitment to justice. Now, as the 47th President of the United States, she was ready to lead the nation into its next chapter. The weight of history was heavy, but she carried it with grace, knowing that her story was not just her own, but that of countless others who had fought for the same dream.

The world watched as the sun set on Washington, D.C., casting a warm glow over the Capitol. It was the end of one chapter and the beginning of another—one that promised to be written by a nation united in its diversity and committed to its ideals.

In the days, months, and years to come, Kamala Harris's presidency would be tested in ways both expected and unforeseen. But on this day, Inauguration Day, the promise of what could be shone brightly. It was a day that would be remembered not just for the history that was made, but for the hope it inspired—a hope that would carry the nation forward, together.

Chapter 2: Setting the Agenda

The Dawn of a New Administration

As Kamala Harris stepped into the Oval Office for the first time as President of the United States, the gravity of her new role weighed heavily on her shoulders. The grandeur of the room, steeped in history and power, was a stark reminder of the immense responsibility that now lay in her hands. Yet, Harris was undeterred. She had spent her career preparing for this moment, navigating the complexities of American politics, and standing firm on issues of justice, equity, and governance. Now, as the 47th President, she was ready to chart a course for the nation's future.

The days following her inauguration were a whirlwind of activity. The nation, still reeling from years of political turmoil, economic uncertainty, and social unrest, looked to her for direction. The country's challenges were multifaceted and deeply entrenched, requiring not just bold vision but practical, effective governance. Harris understood that the early days of her administration would set the tone for the years to come, and she was determined to begin with a clear, decisive agenda.

In her first address to the nation from the Oval Office, Harris outlined her administration's top priorities, each reflecting the critical issues facing the United States and the world. Climate change, healthcare reform, racial justice, and rebuilding international alliances were at the forefront of her agenda. These issues were not only central to her campaign but also deeply personal, shaped by her experiences as a woman of color, a public servant, and a global citizen.

Climate Change: A Call to Action

Among the most urgent items on President Harris's agenda was the fight against climate change. The evidence was clear: the planet was in crisis, and immediate, aggressive action was required to avert catastrophic consequences. The Biden administration had made significant strides in rejoining the Paris Agreement and setting ambitious climate goals, but Harris was determined to go further.

In her inaugural address, Harris had declared, "The time for half-measures is over. We must take bold, transformative steps to combat the climate crisis and protect our planet for future generations." This statement set the stage for an administration that would prioritize environmental sustainability in every aspect of governance.

Harris's climate agenda was comprehensive, aiming to address the root causes of global warming while also promoting economic growth and social equity. The cornerstone of her plan was the Green New Deal 2.0, a sweeping policy framework that built upon the original Green New Deal while incorporating new elements to accelerate the transition to a carbon-neutral economy. The plan included substantial investments in renewable energy,

energy efficiency, and green infrastructure, with the goal of achieving net-zero carbon emissions by 2050.

One of the most ambitious aspects of the Green New Deal 2.0 was the proposal for a National Climate Bank, designed to leverage public and private capital to finance clean energy projects across the country. This initiative aimed to create millions of new jobs in the green economy, particularly in communities that had been historically dependent on fossil fuels. By focusing on economic revitalization in these areas, Harris hoped to build broad-based support for her climate agenda, including in regions that had traditionally been skeptical of environmental regulations.

Harris also prioritized international cooperation on climate issues. She appointed a new Climate Czar, a cabinet-level position tasked with coordinating the U.S.'s efforts in global climate negotiations. This role was filled by John Podesta, a seasoned political strategist and climate advocate, who had served as a key advisor during the Obama administration. Podesta's experience and global connections made him the ideal choice to lead the administration's efforts to rebuild trust and cooperation with international partners.

Under Harris's leadership, the U.S. would not only meet its commitments under the Paris Agreement but also push for more ambitious global targets. The administration planned to host a Global Climate Summit within the first year, bringing together world leaders to discuss coordinated actions to reduce greenhouse gas emissions, protect biodiversity, and assist developing nations in transitioning to sustainable economies.

However, Harris knew that tackling climate change would not be without its challenges. The fossil fuel industry, deeply entrenched and politically powerful, posed significant opposition to her agenda. Furthermore, the political landscape in Congress was divided, with Republicans and some moderate Democrats wary of the economic impacts of aggressive climate policies. Harris understood that achieving her goals would require careful negotiation, coalition-building, and, at times, compromise. But she was resolute in her belief that the stakes were too high to allow inaction.

Healthcare Reform: Building on the Affordable Care Act

Healthcare had long been a central issue in American politics, and it remained a top priority for President Harris. As the first woman to hold the presidency, and as someone who had seen firsthand the struggles of families trying to access affordable healthcare, Harris was committed to expanding and improving the healthcare system.

The Harris administration's healthcare agenda was centered around two key objectives: expanding coverage and reducing costs. Harris believed that healthcare was a fundamental right, not a privilege, and that the government had a responsibility to ensure that every American had access to quality care.

Building on the foundation laid by the Affordable Care Act (ACA), Harris proposed the creation of a public option, a government-run health insurance plan that would compete with private insurers. The public option was designed to provide an affordable alternative for those who could not find adequate coverage through the private market, while also driving down costs across the board by increasing competition. This initiative was a nod to the progressive wing of the Democratic Party, which had long advocated for a single-payer system but recognized the political and practical challenges of such a shift.

Harris also sought to address the rising cost of prescription drugs, which had become a significant burden for many Americans, particularly the elderly and those with chronic conditions. She proposed allowing Medicare to negotiate drug prices directly with pharmaceutical companies, a move that was expected to save billions of dollars in healthcare costs. Additionally, her administration planned to cap out-of-pocket expenses for prescription drugs, ensuring that no American would be forced to choose between their medication and other basic needs.

Mental health care was another area of focus for the Harris administration. The COVID-19 pandemic had exacerbated the mental health crisis in the United States, with millions of Americans experiencing increased levels of anxiety, depression, and other mental health issues. Harris proposed significant investments in mental health services, including expanding access to telehealth, increasing funding for mental health professionals, and integrating mental health care into primary care settings.

The administration also prioritized addressing healthcare disparities that disproportionately affected communities of color and low-income populations. Harris announced the creation of the Office of Health Equity within the Department of Health and Human Services, tasked with coordinating efforts to eliminate disparities in healthcare access, quality, and outcomes. This office would work closely with other federal agencies, state and local governments, and community organizations to develop targeted strategies to reduce health inequities.

Despite the comprehensive nature of her healthcare agenda, Harris knew that achieving these reforms would be an uphill battle. The healthcare industry, including insurance companies and pharmaceutical giants, was one of the most powerful lobbies in Washington. Furthermore, the issue of healthcare had long been a partisan flashpoint, with Republicans largely opposed to government intervention in the healthcare market.

Harris's approach to healthcare reform was pragmatic, recognizing the need to build broad-based support while also making meaningful progress. She worked closely with Vice President Tim Walz, who had extensive experience in healthcare policy from his time as a Congressman and Governor of Minnesota. Together, they engaged in outreach efforts to moderate Democrats and Republicans, emphasizing the economic and moral imperative of expanding healthcare access and affordability.

Racial Justice: A Continuation of the Struggle

Racial justice was not just a policy issue for President Harris; it was a personal mission. As a Black woman of South Asian descent, Harris had spent her career advocating for civil rights, criminal justice reform, and social equity. Now, as President, she was determined to use her platform to advance racial justice on a national scale.

The racial justice agenda of the Harris administration was multifaceted, addressing issues of policing, criminal justice, economic inequality, and voting rights. Harris understood that these issues were deeply interconnected and required a holistic approach.

One of the administration's first actions was the introduction of the George Floyd Justice in Policing Act 2.0, an updated version of the bill that had been introduced during the previous administration but had stalled in the Senate. The new version of the bill included provisions to ban chokeholds, end qualified immunity for law enforcement officers, and create a national database of police misconduct. Additionally, it sought to promote community policing initiatives and provide funding for de-escalation training and mental health crisis intervention.

Harris also prioritized criminal justice reform, building on the work she had done as California's Attorney General and as a U.S. Senator. The administration proposed the

Sentencing Reform and Corrections Act, which aimed to reduce mandatory minimum sentences for non-violent offenses, expand alternatives to incarceration, and invest in rehabilitation and reentry programs. Harris was particularly focused on addressing the racial disparities in the criminal justice system, which had disproportionately impacted Black and Brown communities for decades.

Economic justice was another critical component of Harris's racial justice agenda. She recognized that systemic racism extended beyond the criminal justice system and into the economic structures that perpetuated inequality. To address these disparities, the administration proposed a range of initiatives, including expanding access to capital for minority-owned businesses, increasing funding for Historically Black Colleges and Universities (HBCUs), and implementing targeted job training and workforce development programs in underserved communities.

Voting rights were also a top priority for the Harris administration. In the wake of widespread voter suppression efforts, particularly targeting communities of color, Harris was determined to protect and expand the right to vote. The administration supported the passage of the John Lewis Voting Rights Advancement Act, which aimed to restore and strengthen the protections of the Voting Rights Act of 1965. Additionally, Harris proposed automatic voter registration, expanded early voting, and measures to ensure that every eligible American could vote without undue burden or intimidation.

Harris knew that advancing racial justice would require more than just policy changes; it would require a shift in the national conversation. She used her platform as President to speak candidly about the realities of systemic racism, acknowledging the pain and anger that many Americans felt. She called for a national reckoning on race, encouraging open and honest dialogue about the legacy of slavery, segregation, and discrimination in the United States.

However, Harris also recognized the challenges of advancing racial justice in a deeply polarized nation. The issue of race had long been a divisive one, and there were powerful forces that sought to maintain the status quo. Harris faced opposition from conservative lawmakers, who argued that her policies were too radical and that they threatened to exacerbate divisions rather than heal them. She also faced criticism from some progressives, who believed that her proposals did not go far enough.

Despite these challenges, Harris remained committed to her racial justice agenda. She understood that progress would be incremental and that the fight for justice was a long-term struggle. But she also believed that her administration could make meaningful change, building on the work of those who had come before her and paving the way for future generations.

Rebuilding International Alliances

The final pillar of President Harris's agenda was the restoration and strengthening of international alliances.

MADAM PRESIDENT: THE FIRST TERM OF KAMALA HARRIS

After years of tension and disengagement from global institutions, Harris was determined to rebuild America's standing in the world and reaffirm its commitment to multilateralism.

The Harris administration's foreign policy was guided by the principle of "Smart Power," which emphasized the use of diplomacy, development, and defense in a balanced and coordinated manner. Harris believed that the United States could not afford to retreat from the world stage, but that its engagement needed to be more strategic, cooperative, and aligned with global values.

One of the first actions taken by the Harris administration was to reassert America's leadership in global climate negotiations. Harris appointed a special envoy for climate, tasked with coordinating U.S. efforts in international climate talks and working with other countries to achieve ambitious emissions reduction targets. The administration also pledged to increase funding for climate adaptation and resilience in developing countries, recognizing that the impacts of climate change were felt most acutely by the world's poorest and most vulnerable populations.

Harris also prioritized rebuilding alliances with traditional partners in Europe and Asia. She made it clear that the United States would stand by its commitments to NATO and work to strengthen transatlantic relations. At the same time, the administration sought to deepen ties with key allies in the Asia-Pacific region, particularly in the face of an increasingly assertive China.

Trade was another area of focus for the Harris administration. Harris believed in the importance of fair and open trade, but she also recognized the need to address the concerns of American workers and industries that had been adversely affected by globalization. The administration sought to renegotiate trade agreements to include stronger labor and environmental standards, and to protect key industries while promoting innovation and competitiveness.

Human rights and democracy were also central to Harris's foreign policy agenda. The administration took a strong stance against authoritarianism, supporting pro-democracy movements in countries like Belarus, Myanmar, and Hong Kong. Harris made it clear that the United States would not turn a blind eye to human rights abuses, and that it would use its influence to promote freedom, justice, and equality around the world.

However, rebuilding international alliances was not without its challenges. The world had changed significantly over the past decade, and America's global standing had been eroded by years of disengagement and inconsistent foreign policy. Harris faced skepticism from some international partners, who questioned whether the United States could be trusted to maintain its commitments. There were also tensions with rival powers, particularly China and Russia, who viewed America's renewed engagement as a threat to their own ambitions.

To navigate these challenges, Harris relied on a seasoned team of foreign policy experts, many of whom had served in previous administrations. She appointed Antony Blinken as Secretary of State, a diplomat with deep experience and a strong commitment to multilateralism. Jake Sullivan, who had served as National Security Advisor under Biden, was brought back in the same role, providing continuity and strategic vision. Harris also appointed Samantha Power, a former U.S. Ambassador to the United Nations, to lead the U.S. Agency for International Development (USAID), emphasizing the importance of development in American foreign policy.

Together, this team worked to restore America's credibility and influence on the global stage. They engaged in extensive diplomatic outreach, rebuilding trust with allies and partners, and addressing the concerns of countries that had been alienated by previous administrations. Harris herself was an active participant in these efforts, making frequent calls to foreign leaders, attending international summits, and delivering speeches that articulated America's vision for a more just and cooperative world.

Building the Cabinet and Key Advisors

One of President Harris's first tasks upon taking office was assembling her Cabinet and key advisors. She was committed to building a team that reflected the diversity and talent of the American people, while also bringing in experienced and capable leaders who could execute her ambitious agenda.

Harris's Cabinet was notable for its diversity, with women, people of color, and individuals from a wide range of backgrounds holding key positions. This diversity was not just symbolic; it was a deliberate choice to ensure that the voices of all Americans were represented at the highest levels of government.

Among the most significant appointments was Janet Yellen as Secretary of the Treasury. Yellen, who had previously served as Chair of the Federal Reserve, was widely respected for her expertise in economic policy. She was tasked with guiding the administration's efforts to rebuild the economy, address income inequality, and ensure fiscal stability.

Lloyd Austin was appointed as Secretary of Defense, making him the first African American to lead the Pentagon. Austin, a retired four-star general, brought decades of military experience and a deep understanding of national security issues. Harris believed that Austin's leadership would be critical in modernizing the military and addressing emerging threats, including cyber warfare and climate-related security challenges.

Deb Haaland, a member of the Laguna Pueblo tribe, was appointed Secretary of the Interior, making her the first Native American to lead the department. Haaland's appointment was a historic milestone and reflected Harris's commitment to protecting the environment and upholding the rights of Indigenous peoples. Haaland was tasked with overseeing the administration's efforts to conserve public lands, promote renewable energy development, and address the impacts of climate change on natural resources.

Other notable appointments included Xavier Becerra as Secretary of Health and Human Services, tasked with overseeing the administration's healthcare reforms; Alejandro Mayorkas as Secretary of Homeland Security, responsible for managing immigration policy and national security; and Merrick Garland as Attorney General, charged with upholding the rule of law and pursuing justice for all Americans.

In addition to her Cabinet, Harris assembled a team of key advisors who would play critical roles in shaping and implementing her agenda. Susan Rice, a former National Security Advisor and U.N. Ambassador, was appointed as Director of the Domestic Policy Council, where she would oversee the administration's efforts on issues such as healthcare, education, and racial justice. Ron Klain, who had served as Chief of Staff to President Biden, was brought back in the same role, providing continuity and experience in managing the complexities of the White House.

Harris also appointed a diverse and talented group of special advisors and senior staff, many of whom were women and people of color. This team included individuals with deep expertise in areas such as climate change, economic policy, technology, and social justice. Harris believed that their insights and perspectives would be essential in addressing the complex challenges facing the nation.

Challenges in Forming a Bipartisan Coalition

While Harris was committed to advancing her ambitious agenda, she was also acutely aware of the challenges she faced in navigating a deeply divided Congress. The 2024 elections had left the House of Representatives narrowly controlled by Democrats, while the Senate was split 50-50, with Vice President Tim Walz holding the tie-breaking vote. This razor-thin margin meant that Harris would need to build a bipartisan coalition to pass any significant legislation.

Harris knew that achieving her policy goals would require careful negotiation, compromise, and coalition-building. She was determined to avoid the gridlock that had plagued previous administrations and was committed to working with lawmakers on both sides of the aisle to find common ground.

One of the first challenges Harris faced was the confirmation of her Cabinet and key appointments. While most of her nominees were ultimately confirmed, the process was contentious, with several Republican senators expressing concerns about the administration's agenda and the ideological leanings of some nominees. Harris and her team engaged in extensive outreach to moderate Republicans, emphasizing the qualifications and experience of her nominees and the importance of a functioning government.

The confirmation process was a reminder of the challenges Harris would face in advancing her legislative agenda. She knew that passing major reforms on issues such as climate change, healthcare, and racial justice would require building a coalition that included not only progressive Democrats but also moderates and Republicans.

To that end, Harris worked closely with Vice President Walz, who had a reputation for bipartisanship from his time in Congress and as Governor of Minnesota. Walz played a key role in reaching out to moderate Democrats and Republicans, using his relationships and political capital to build support for the administration's agenda.

Harris also sought to build relationships with key leaders in Congress, including Senate Majority Leader Chuck Schumer and House Speaker Hakeem Jeffries. She understood the importance of maintaining open lines of communication and was committed to working closely with congressional leaders to navigate the legislative process.

However, Harris also faced opposition from conservative Republicans, who were deeply skeptical of her agenda and determined to block her initiatives. Senate Minority Leader Mitch McConnell and other Republican leaders signaled their intention to oppose many of the administration's key proposals, particularly on issues such as climate change and healthcare.

Harris knew that achieving her goals would require not just negotiation but also public support. She embarked on a nationwide tour to build momentum for her agenda, visiting key swing states and engaging directly with voters. She held town halls, roundtable discussions, and community events, listening to the concerns of ordinary Americans and making the case for her policies.

Harris also sought to leverage the power of social media and digital outreach to communicate directly with the American people. She used platforms like Twitter, Facebook, and Instagram to share updates on her administration's progress, highlight the stories of those impacted by her policies, and counter misinformation.

Despite the challenges, Harris remained optimistic about the potential for bipartisan cooperation. She believed that most Americans, regardless of political affiliation, wanted to see progress on issues like healthcare, climate change, and racial justice. She was committed to working with lawmakers on both sides of the aisle to find solutions that would benefit all Americans.

As President Kamala Harris began her first term in office, she was guided by a clear and ambitious agenda. Climate change, healthcare reform, racial justice, and rebuilding international alliances were at the forefront of her priorities, reflecting the critical issues facing the United States and the world.

Harris knew that achieving her goals would not be easy. She faced significant challenges, including a divided Congress, powerful special interests, and deep-seated political divisions. But she was determined to govern with a spirit of collaboration, pragmatism, and unwavering commitment to justice and equity.

MADAM PRESIDENT: THE FIRST TERM OF KAMALA HARRIS

In the early days of her administration, Harris took decisive steps to set the agenda, appointing a diverse and talented team, engaging in outreach to build bipartisan support, and communicating directly with the American people. While the road ahead was uncertain, Harris was prepared to lead the nation through the challenges and opportunities of the 21st century.

Her presidency was not just about the policies she would enact but about the vision she embodied—a vision of an America that was more just, more inclusive, and more united. As she looked ahead to the work that lay before her, Harris knew that the legacy of her administration would be shaped not only by the decisions she made but by the progress she achieved in building a better future for all Americans.

Chapter 3: Confronting the Pandemic

The Enduring Threat of COVID-19

As Kamala Harris assumed the presidency, one of the most pressing challenges she faced was the ongoing battle against COVID-19. Though the worst waves of the pandemic had passed by the time she took office in January 2025, the virus was far from eradicated. New variants had emerged, some more transmissible and deadlier than earlier strains, threatening the progress made by previous administrations in controlling the spread. The virus remained a potent force of disruption, impacting public health, the economy, and the fabric of society.

The COVID-19 pandemic had redefined what it meant to govern, forcing leaders to prioritize public health, balance civil liberties with emergency measures, and manage the profound economic fallout. For Harris, the challenge was not just about containing the virus but also about addressing the long-term consequences that the pandemic had wrought on a weary nation and a world that had grown increasingly interconnected yet vulnerable.

Her administration would be tasked with continuing the work of vaccination, dealing with emerging variants, strengthening the public health infrastructure, and rebuilding a society that had been altered by more than four years of living with the constant threat of a pandemic. Harris knew that her leadership in this fight would define not only her presidency but also the future resilience of the United States.

The New Variants: A Renewed Threat

Just as Harris was settling into her role as President, scientists sounded the alarm over several new variants of the COVID-19 virus. These variants, identified in various parts of the world, were more resistant to the existing vaccines, leading to a surge in cases and hospitalizations. The emergence of these new strains posed a significant challenge to the global effort to bring the pandemic under control.

The Harris administration immediately convened a task force of top epidemiologists, virologists, and public health officials to assess the situation and develop a strategy to address the new variants. This task force, led by Dr. Rochelle Walensky, who had served as Director of the Centers for Disease Control and Prevention (CDC) under President Biden, and Dr. Anthony Fauci, the nation's leading infectious disease expert, was charged with coordinating the federal response to the evolving threat.

One of the first actions taken by the administration was to ramp up genomic surveillance efforts to track the spread of the new variants. This involved increasing funding for labs to sequence more virus samples, as well as collaborating with international partners to share data and monitor the global spread of these variants. The administration also prioritized the development and approval of updated vaccines that could provide protection against the new strains.

Harris understood that the public was exhausted from years of dealing with the pandemic. There was widespread "pandemic fatigue," and many Americans were eager to return to normalcy. However, Harris was committed to ensuring that the nation did not let its guard down. She urged the public to continue following public health guidelines, including mask-wearing and social distancing, even as vaccinations continued.

In her first major public address on the pandemic, Harris struck a tone of both empathy and resolve. She acknowledged the hardships that Americans had endured—the loss of loved ones, the economic hardships, the disruption to everyday life—but she also emphasized the need for continued vigilance.

"We have come too far and sacrificed too much to falter now," she said. "We must remain vigilant, we must remain united, and we must remain committed to protecting one another. The fight against COVID-19 is not over, but together, we can and will overcome this challenge."

Harris's message resonated with many Americans who had grown weary of the pandemic's toll. She understood that leadership in this moment required not only policy decisions but also the ability to inspire hope and resilience in the face of adversity.

Accelerating Vaccine Distribution Globally

One of the key pillars of Harris's strategy to combat the pandemic was to accelerate vaccine distribution, both domestically and globally. The emergence of new variants highlighted the importance of achieving widespread immunity, not just in the United States but around the world. Harris believed that the pandemic could not be fully controlled unless the virus was brought under control globally.

The previous administration had made significant progress in vaccinating the American population, with over 80% of adults receiving at least one dose of the vaccine by the time Harris took office. However, the global vaccination effort had been uneven, with many low- and middle-income countries struggling to secure sufficient vaccine supplies. This disparity had created conditions where the virus could continue to mutate and spread, posing a threat to everyone, regardless of national borders.

Harris, therefore, prioritized global vaccine distribution as a central component of her administration's pandemic response. She announced a bold new initiative, the Global Vaccine Equity Partnership (GVEP), aimed at ensuring that every country, regardless of its economic status, had access to COVID-19 vaccines. The initiative was a multilateral effort, bringing together governments, international organizations, non-profits, and the private sector to coordinate the distribution of vaccines to underserved regions.

The GVEP was designed to address several key challenges in the global vaccination effort. First, it sought to increase vaccine production by providing funding and technical support to manufacturers in developing countries. This included expanding manufacturing capacity in regions like Africa, Latin America, and Southeast Asia, which had been heavily reliant on imports from a few major producers.

Second, the initiative focused on logistics and distribution, ensuring that vaccines could be safely transported and stored in even the most remote and resource-limited settings. This involved investing in cold chain infrastructure, training healthcare workers, and providing the necessary supplies, such as syringes and personal protective equipment.

Third, the GVEP aimed to combat vaccine hesitancy by launching public awareness campaigns and providing accurate, culturally sensitive information about the safety and efficacy of the vaccines. Harris recognized that misinformation and distrust in vaccines were significant barriers to achieving global vaccination targets, and she was determined to address these issues head-on.

The GVEP was met with widespread support from the international community. The World Health Organization (WHO), the United Nations, and key global health organizations such as Gavi, the Vaccine Alliance, and the Coalition for Epidemic Preparedness Innovations (CEPI) were key partners in the effort. Major pharmaceutical companies also committed to participating in the initiative, with some agreeing to share technology and waive patent rights to facilitate the production of generic vaccines.

Harris's leadership in global vaccine distribution was seen as a critical step in restoring the United States' standing as a global leader in public health. After years of retreating from international cooperation under previous administrations, Harris was determined to reassert the U.S. as a force for good on the world stage.

Domestically, Harris continued the push to vaccinate as many Americans as possible, with a focus on reaching underserved and hesitant communities. The administration expanded mobile vaccination units, increased funding for community health centers, and worked with local leaders and organizations to address concerns and misinformation about the vaccines.

Harris also took steps to ensure that the vaccines were updated to address new variants. The administration worked closely with vaccine manufacturers to accelerate the development and approval of booster shots and updated vaccines that could provide stronger protection against emerging strains. By staying ahead of the virus and adapting to its evolution, Harris aimed to prevent future surges and move the country closer to a post-pandemic reality.

Strengthening Public Health Infrastructure

The COVID-19 pandemic had exposed significant weaknesses in the United States' public health infrastructure. Years of underfunding, combined with the unprecedented scale of the pandemic, had left the system struggling to respond effectively. As President, Harris recognized the need to not only address the immediate crisis but also to strengthen the public health system to ensure the country was better prepared for future pandemics and health emergencies.

One of the administration's first actions was to secure funding for the Public Health Emergency Fund, which had been depleted during the initial waves of the pandemic. Harris worked with Congress to pass a comprehensive public health infrastructure bill, which provided billions of dollars in funding to state and local health departments, hospitals, and other critical institutions. This funding was aimed at bolstering the nation's ability to respond to future health crises, including pandemics, natural disasters, and bioterrorism threats.

The bill also included provisions to modernize the nation's public health data systems. The pandemic had highlighted the need for real-time data collection and analysis to guide decision-making. Harris's administration invested in upgrading outdated systems, integrating electronic health records, and improving data sharing between federal, state, and local agencies. These efforts were designed to create a more agile and responsive public health system that could quickly identify and respond to emerging threats.

In addition to infrastructure improvements, Harris prioritized expanding the public health workforce. The administration launched the Public Health Corps, a new initiative aimed at recruiting and training thousands of public health professionals, including epidemiologists, contact tracers, and community health workers. This corps was designed to be rapidly deployable in the event of future outbreaks, ensuring that communities had the resources they needed to contain and manage health crises.

Harris also focused on addressing health disparities that had been exacerbated by the pandemic. The administration created the Health Equity Task Force, which was tasked with identifying and addressing the social determinants of health that contributed to higher rates of illness and death in communities of color. This task force worked closely with the Office of Health Equity within the Department of Health and Human Services (HHS) to develop targeted interventions, such as increasing access to healthcare, improving housing conditions, and addressing food insecurity.

In addition to these initiatives, Harris recognized the need to reform the nation's healthcare system to better align it with public health goals. The administration pushed for the integration of public health and primary care, with a focus on prevention and early intervention. Harris also supported the expansion of telehealth services, which had proven to be a valuable tool during the pandemic, particularly in reaching rural and underserved populations.

The administration's efforts to strengthen public health infrastructure were widely praised by public health experts, who recognized the importance of building a system that could not only respond to the current pandemic but also prevent and mitigate future health crises.

Harris's approach was seen as a long-overdue investment in the nation's health and well-being.

Addressing the Long-Term Impacts of the Pandemic

While the immediate focus of the Harris administration was on controlling the spread of COVID-19 and strengthening public health infrastructure, Harris also understood that the pandemic had far-reaching impacts that would need to be addressed in the long term. The economic, social, and psychological toll of the pandemic was immense, and Harris was committed to leading the nation through a comprehensive recovery.

One of the most significant long-term impacts of the pandemic was the economic disruption it had caused. Millions of Americans had lost their jobs, businesses had closed, and entire industries had been upended. The economic recovery under the Biden administration had been uneven, with some sectors rebounding while others continued to struggle. Harris recognized that a full economic recovery would require a multi-faceted approach that addressed both immediate needs and long-term structural issues.

The administration's economic recovery plan, known as the American Recovery and Resilience Act, was a comprehensive package aimed at rebuilding the economy and addressing the inequalities that had been exacerbated by the pandemic. The plan included significant investments in infrastructure, education, and job training, with a focus on creating good-paying jobs in sectors such as renewable energy, technology, and healthcare.

Harris also prioritized support for small businesses, which had been particularly hard-hit by the pandemic. The administration expanded loan and grant programs, provided technical assistance, and worked to reduce barriers to entry for minority-owned businesses. By supporting entrepreneurship and innovation, Harris aimed to foster a more resilient and inclusive economy.

Another key aspect of the recovery plan was addressing the long-term impacts on education. The pandemic had caused significant disruptions to education, with many students experiencing learning loss due to school closures and the shift to remote learning. The administration launched the Learning Recovery Initiative, which provided funding for tutoring, summer programs, and mental health support for students. Harris also prioritized closing the digital divide, recognizing that access to technology and the internet was essential for students to succeed in a post-pandemic world.

In addition to economic and educational impacts, Harris was deeply concerned about the mental health crisis that had emerged during the pandemic. The prolonged stress, isolation, and uncertainty had taken a toll on the mental well-being of millions of Americans. The administration's mental health strategy included expanding access to mental health services, increasing funding for research and treatment, and launching public awareness campaigns to reduce stigma and encourage people to seek help.

Harris also recognized the importance of addressing the social and emotional impacts of the pandemic. The administration supported community-based initiatives that promoted social connectedness and resilience, particularly in communities that had been disproportionately affected by the virus. Harris believed that healing the nation's social fabric was essential for a full recovery and that the government had a role to play in supporting these efforts.

In addition to these domestic efforts, Harris was also focused on the global impacts of the pandemic. The economic and social disruption caused by COVID-19 had been felt around the world, particularly in developing countries. The administration worked with international partners to provide economic assistance, debt relief, and support for global recovery efforts. Harris believed that a coordinated global response was essential for ensuring a more equitable and sustainable recovery.

Looking Ahead: Building a Resilient Future

As President Harris continued to lead the nation through the challenges of the COVID-19 pandemic, she remained focused on the future. The pandemic had exposed the vulnerabilities of the global system and underscored the need for greater resilience in the face of future threats.

Harris's vision for a post-pandemic world was one in which the United States and the international community were better prepared for future pandemics, natural disasters, and other global challenges. She believed that building resilience required not only strengthening public health systems but also addressing the root causes of vulnerability, such as inequality, environmental degradation, and weak governance.

To that end, Harris supported the creation of a Global Resilience Fund, a new international initiative aimed at building the capacity of countries to respond to future crises. The fund provided resources for strengthening health systems, improving infrastructure, and supporting sustainable development. Harris believed that investing in resilience was not only a moral imperative but also a strategic one, as it would reduce the likelihood of future crises and mitigate their impacts when they did occur.

Domestically, Harris continued to push for policies that promoted resilience in all aspects of society. She supported efforts to build resilient infrastructure, such as investing in renewable energy and climate adaptation measures. She also advocated for social policies that promoted equity and inclusion, recognizing that a more just society was a more resilient one.

As she looked ahead, Harris knew that the work of building resilience was an ongoing process. The COVID-19 pandemic had been a wake-up call for the world, highlighting the need for greater cooperation, innovation, and preparedness. Harris was committed to leading the United States through this process, ensuring that the nation emerged from the pandemic stronger, more united, and better equipped to face the challenges of the future.

Confronting the COVID-19 pandemic was one of the most significant challenges of President Kamala Harris's early days in office. The virus, with its evolving variants, continued to threaten public health, disrupt economies, and strain the social fabric of the nation and the world. Yet, under Harris's leadership, the United States took bold and decisive action to combat the virus, strengthen public health infrastructure, and address the long-term impacts of the pandemic.

Harris's approach to the pandemic was characterized by a commitment to science, equity, and global cooperation. She recognized that the fight against COVID-19 was not just about managing a public health crisis but about building a more resilient and just society. Through initiatives such as the Global Vaccine Equity Partnership, the Public Health Corps, and the American Recovery and Resilience Act, Harris laid the foundation for a recovery that was not only about returning to normal but about creating a better future.

As the nation continued to navigate the challenges of the pandemic, Harris's leadership provided a sense of direction, hope, and determination. She understood that the road to recovery would be long and that the fight against COVID-19 was far from over. But she also believed that by working together, the United States and the world could overcome this challenge and emerge stronger and more resilient.

In the years to come, the legacy of Harris's pandemic response would be measured not only by the number of lives saved but by the lasting changes it brought to public health, the economy, and society. Her administration's efforts to confront the pandemic were a testament to the power of leadership, the importance of science, and the resilience of the human spirit in the face of adversity.

Chapter 4: Economic Recovery and Innovation

The Challenge of Economic Recovery

When Kamala Harris assumed the presidency, the United States was still grappling with the lingering economic effects of the COVID-19 pandemic. While the country had made significant strides toward recovery during the latter part of the Biden administration, the economy remained fragile. Millions of Americans were still out of work, small businesses were struggling to stay afloat, and entire industries were facing the prospect of permanent decline. In addition to these immediate challenges, there were longer-term structural issues—rising inequality, stagnant wages, and an aging infrastructure—that required urgent attention.

President Harris understood that her administration's success would be judged in large part by its ability to deliver a robust and equitable economic recovery. But she also recognized that recovery alone was not enough. The goal was not simply to return to the pre-pandemic status quo but to build a stronger, more resilient, and more inclusive economy for the future. This vision was encapsulated in the "Build Back Better" economic recovery plan, which aimed to address the immediate needs of the economy while laying the foundation for long-term prosperity.

MADAM PRESIDENT: THE FIRST TERM OF KAMALA HARRIS

The "Build Back Better" plan was both ambitious and comprehensive, focusing on green jobs, infrastructure investment, and technological innovation. Harris believed that by investing in these areas, the United States could not only accelerate its recovery but also position itself as a global leader in the 21st century economy. However, the plan also faced significant challenges, including the need to balance economic growth with concerns about inflation and budget deficits.

The Vision of "Build Back Better"

At the heart of the "Build Back Better" plan was a vision of an economy that was not only prosperous but also equitable, sustainable, and resilient. Harris believed that the economic recovery needed to be more than just a short-term fix; it needed to address the systemic issues that had left so many Americans vulnerable to the pandemic's economic fallout. This meant focusing on creating good-paying jobs, reducing inequality, and ensuring that the benefits of economic growth were broadly shared.

One of the key pillars of the plan was the transition to a green economy. Harris had long been a champion of environmental sustainability, and she saw the post-pandemic recovery as an opportunity to accelerate the shift away from fossil fuels and toward renewable energy. The administration proposed massive investments in clean energy infrastructure, including wind, solar, and electric vehicle charging stations. These investments were designed to create millions of new jobs in the green economy while reducing the nation's carbon footprint and combating climate change.

In addition to green energy, the "Build Back Better" plan called for significant investments in infrastructure. The United States' infrastructure—its roads, bridges, railways, and water systems—had been neglected for decades, leading to crumbling facilities and costly inefficiencies. Harris's plan aimed to address these issues by funding a wide range of infrastructure projects, from repairing aging bridges to expanding broadband access in rural areas. The goal was not only to modernize the nation's infrastructure but also to create jobs and stimulate economic activity in communities across the country.

Another major focus of the "Build Back Better" plan was technological innovation. Harris believed that the future of the U.S. economy depended on its ability to lead in emerging technologies, such as artificial intelligence, quantum computing, and biotechnology. The administration proposed significant funding for research and development, as well as support for startups and small businesses in the tech sector. By fostering innovation, Harris aimed to ensure that the United States remained competitive in the global economy and that Americans had access to the high-paying jobs of the future.

However, Harris was also keenly aware of the need to balance these ambitious investments with fiscal responsibility. The "Build Back Better" plan included measures to address the federal budget deficit, which had ballooned during the pandemic due to emergency spending on relief programs. Harris proposed a combination of tax reforms, including raising taxes on the wealthiest Americans and corporations, and spending cuts in other areas to ensure that the plan was fiscally sustainable.

Green Jobs and the Transition to a Sustainable Economy

One of the most significant aspects of the "Build Back Better" plan was its emphasis on green jobs and the transition to a sustainable economy. Harris believed that addressing climate change was not only an environmental imperative but also an economic opportunity. By investing in renewable energy and other sustainable industries, the United States could create millions of new jobs, reduce its reliance on fossil fuels, and position itself as a leader in the global green economy.

The Harris administration's green jobs strategy focused on several key areas: renewable energy, energy efficiency, electric vehicles, and sustainable agriculture. Each of these areas was targeted for significant investment and support, with the goal of creating a robust and diverse green economy that could provide good-paying jobs for Americans across the country.

Renewable Energy: Powering the Future

The centerpiece of the green jobs strategy was the expansion of renewable energy. Harris's plan called for a massive increase in the production of wind and solar power, with the goal of generating 100% of the nation's electricity from clean energy sources by 2050. To achieve this, the administration proposed significant investments in wind and solar farms, as well as in the infrastructure needed to connect these energy sources to the grid.

One of the administration's first actions was to restore and expand the Production Tax Credit (PTC) and the Investment Tax Credit (ITC) for renewable energy projects. These tax credits had been critical in driving the growth of the renewable energy sector in the past, and Harris believed that extending them would provide the financial certainty needed to spur further investment.

In addition to tax incentives, the administration also provided grants and low-interest loans to support the development of renewable energy projects, particularly in underserved and economically distressed areas. The goal was to ensure that the benefits of the green economy were broadly shared and that all Americans had access to clean, affordable energy.

The administration's efforts quickly began to bear fruit. By the end of Harris's first year in office, the renewable energy sector had seen significant growth, with new wind and solar projects breaking ground across the country. The construction of these projects created tens of thousands of jobs, many of them in rural areas that had been struggling with economic decline.

In addition to job creation, the expansion of renewable energy also had significant environmental benefits. As more wind and solar power came online, the United States saw a reduction in greenhouse gas emissions, helping to move the country closer to its climate goals.

Energy Efficiency: Reducing Waste and Saving Money

Another key component of the green jobs strategy was energy efficiency. Harris believed that improving energy efficiency was one of the most cost-effective ways to reduce greenhouse gas emissions and lower energy costs for consumers. The administration's plan included a wide range of initiatives aimed at making homes, businesses, and public buildings more energy-efficient.

One of the administration's flagship programs was the Green Homes Initiative, which provided grants and low-interest loans to homeowners and landlords to retrofit their properties with energy-efficient technologies. This included installing insulation, upgrading heating and cooling systems, and replacing old windows and doors with energy-efficient models. The program also provided incentives for the installation of solar panels and other renewable energy systems on residential properties.

The Green Homes Initiative was particularly beneficial for low- and moderate-income households, many of whom lived in older, less energy-efficient homes. By reducing energy consumption, the program helped these families save money on their utility bills while also reducing their carbon footprint.

In addition to residential energy efficiency, the administration also focused on making public buildings more energy-efficient. The Green Schools Program provided funding to schools and universities to upgrade their facilities, with a focus on improving indoor air quality and reducing energy consumption. The program not only created jobs in the construction and building trades but also provided students with healthier learning environments.

The administration also targeted energy efficiency in the industrial sector. The Green Manufacturing Initiative provided grants and tax incentives to companies that implemented energy-efficient practices and technologies in their manufacturing processes. This included everything from upgrading machinery to using renewable energy to power factories. By improving energy efficiency, these companies were able to reduce their operating costs, making them more competitive in the global market.

The combined impact of these energy efficiency initiatives was significant. By the end of Harris's first term, the United States had made substantial progress in reducing its overall energy consumption, saving billions of dollars in energy costs and reducing greenhouse gas emissions. The energy efficiency sector also became a major source of job growth, with thousands of new jobs created in retrofitting, construction, and manufacturing.

Electric Vehicles: Driving the Future

The Harris administration also made the promotion of electric vehicles (EVs) a central component of its green jobs strategy. Harris believed that the widespread adoption of EVs was essential for reducing greenhouse gas emissions from the transportation sector, which was one of the largest sources of carbon pollution in the United States.

The administration's plan included a wide range of incentives and investments aimed at accelerating the transition to electric vehicles. One of the key initiatives was the EV Rebate Program, which provided financial incentives to consumers who purchased electric vehicles. The program offered rebates of up to $7,500 for new EVs and up to $4,000 for used EVs, making electric vehicles more affordable for a wider range of consumers.

In addition to consumer incentives, the administration also invested in the expansion of the nation's EV charging infrastructure. The Electric Highway Initiative provided funding for the installation of fast-charging stations along major highways and in urban centers, ensuring that drivers could easily charge their vehicles on long trips. The administration also worked with utility companies and local governments to expand charging infrastructure in residential areas, workplaces, and public parking lots.

The administration's efforts to promote electric vehicles were supported by significant investments in the domestic manufacturing of EVs and their components. The Electric Vehicle Supply Chain Initiative provided grants and tax incentives to companies that produced batteries, electric motors, and other critical components in the United States. The goal was to build

a robust domestic supply chain for EVs, reducing the country's reliance on imports and creating jobs in the manufacturing sector.

The results of these efforts were impressive. By the end of Harris's first term, the number of electric vehicles on the road had more than doubled, and the United States had become a global leader in EV manufacturing. The expansion of the EV market created tens of thousands of new jobs in the automotive and related industries, from manufacturing to charging infrastructure installation.

The widespread adoption of electric vehicles also had significant environmental benefits. As more consumers switched to EVs, the United States saw a reduction in greenhouse gas emissions from the transportation sector, helping to move the country closer to its climate goals.

Sustainable Agriculture: Feeding the Future

The Harris administration also recognized the importance of promoting sustainable agriculture as part of its green jobs strategy. Agriculture was both a major contributor to greenhouse gas emissions and a sector that was particularly vulnerable to the impacts of climate change. Harris believed that by supporting sustainable farming practices, the United States could reduce its environmental footprint, improve food security, and create jobs in rural areas.

The administration's plan included a range of initiatives aimed at promoting sustainable agriculture and supporting farmers who adopted environmentally friendly practices. One of the key programs was the Sustainable Agriculture Grants Program, which provided financial assistance to farmers and ranchers who implemented practices such as cover cropping, no-till farming, and rotational grazing. These practices helped to sequester carbon in the soil, reduce erosion, and improve water quality.

The administration also promoted the expansion of organic farming, which had a lower environmental impact than conventional agriculture. The Organic Transition Program provided grants and technical assistance to farmers who wanted to transition to organic production, as well as support for certification and marketing. The program aimed to increase the availability of organic products for consumers while providing farmers with higher-value markets.

In addition to promoting sustainable farming practices, the administration also focused on reducing food waste and supporting local food systems. The Food Waste Reduction Initiative provided funding for programs that diverted surplus food to food banks and other organizations that served people in need. The Local Food Promotion Program supported farmers markets, food hubs, and other initiatives that connected consumers with local producers.

The administration's efforts to promote sustainable agriculture were met with widespread support from the farming community, environmental organizations, and consumers. By the end of Harris's first term, the United States had made significant progress in reducing the environmental impact of agriculture, improving soil health, and supporting the livelihoods of farmers and ranchers.

Balancing Economic Recovery with Inflation and Budget Deficits

While the "Build Back Better" plan was ambitious and comprehensive, it also faced significant challenges, particularly in the areas of inflation and budget deficits. The massive investments required to implement the plan, combined with the economic disruptions caused by the pandemic, created concerns about rising inflation and the sustainability of the federal budget.

Inflation had become a growing concern by the time Harris took office. The pandemic had caused supply chain disruptions, labor shortages, and increased demand for goods and services, all of which contributed to rising prices. While the Federal Reserve had taken steps to manage inflation, there were fears that the administration's large-scale spending could exacerbate the problem.

Harris and her economic team, led by Treasury Secretary Janet Yellen, were acutely aware of these concerns. They sought to balance the need for economic recovery with the imperative of keeping inflation under control. One of the key strategies was to phase in spending gradually, focusing on immediate needs first while delaying some of the longer-term investments until the economy had stabilized.

The administration also worked closely with the Federal Reserve to ensure that monetary policy was aligned with fiscal policy. Harris maintained regular communication with Federal Reserve Chair Jerome Powell, emphasizing the importance of managing inflation while supporting economic growth. The Fed, in turn, used its tools to manage interest rates and control inflation, while signaling its willingness to adjust policy as needed.

Another major concern was the federal budget deficit, which had ballooned during the pandemic due to emergency spending on relief programs. Harris was committed to addressing the deficit, but she also believed that austerity measures could undermine the recovery. Instead, the administration focused on a combination of tax reforms and targeted spending cuts to ensure fiscal sustainability.

The tax reforms proposed by the Harris administration included raising taxes on the wealthiest Americans and corporations, closing loopholes, and cracking down on tax evasion. These measures were designed to generate additional revenue without placing an undue burden on middle-class and working-class families. The administration also proposed a new minimum tax on multinational corporations, aimed at preventing companies from shifting profits to low-tax jurisdictions.

On the spending side, the administration identified areas where cuts could be made without undermining essential services or investments in the future. This included reducing subsidies for fossil fuel industries, cutting wasteful defense spending, and streamlining government operations to improve efficiency.

Despite these efforts, the challenges of balancing economic recovery with inflation and budget deficits remained significant. The administration faced criticism from both the left and the right, with some progressives arguing that the spending cuts were too harsh, while conservatives warned that the tax increases could stifle economic growth.

Harris and her team navigated these challenges by emphasizing the long-term benefits of the "Build Back Better" plan. They argued that the investments in green jobs, infrastructure, and innovation would create a stronger, more resilient economy, generating growth and revenue that would help to offset the costs. The administration also highlighted the importance of addressing climate change and inequality, which they believed were not just moral imperatives but also essential for long-term economic stability.

Success Stories: New Industries and a Focus on Sustainability

As the "Build Back Better" plan was implemented, it began to yield tangible results, particularly in the areas of job creation, innovation, and sustainability. The investments in green jobs, infrastructure, and technological innovation led to the emergence of new industries and the revitalization of existing ones, creating a more dynamic and sustainable economy.

MADAM PRESIDENT: THE FIRST TERM OF KAMALA HARRIS

One of the most notable success stories was the rapid growth of the renewable energy sector. The administration's investments in wind and solar power, combined with the restoration of tax credits and the expansion of domestic manufacturing, led to a boom in renewable energy projects across the country. By the end of Harris's first term, the United States had become a global leader in renewable energy production, creating hundreds of thousands of new jobs and reducing the nation's reliance on fossil fuels.

The electric vehicle (EV) industry also experienced significant growth. The combination of consumer incentives, expanded charging infrastructure, and support for domestic manufacturing led to a surge in EV sales and production. The United States became one of the largest markets for electric vehicles, with new models being developed and produced by both established automakers and startups. The expansion of the EV market created tens of thousands of jobs in manufacturing, technology, and infrastructure, while also reducing greenhouse gas emissions from the transportation sector.

In addition to renewable energy and electric vehicles, the administration's focus on technological innovation led to the emergence of new industries and advancements in existing ones. The significant funding for research and development, combined with support for startups and small businesses, fostered innovation in areas such as artificial intelligence, quantum computing, biotechnology, and clean technology.

One of the most promising new industries was the development of advanced battery technology. The administration's investments in research and manufacturing led to significant breakthroughs in battery efficiency and storage capacity, which had applications not only in electric vehicles but also in renewable energy storage and grid management. The growth of the battery industry created new jobs and positioned the United States as a leader in a critical technology for the future.

Another success story was the revitalization of American manufacturing. The administration's focus on rebuilding domestic supply chains, combined with investments in energy efficiency and innovation, led to a resurgence in manufacturing across the country. New factories were built to produce electric vehicles, renewable energy components, and advanced technologies, creating jobs and stimulating economic growth in regions that had been left behind by globalization.

The administration's efforts to promote sustainable agriculture also yielded positive results. The support for organic farming, sustainable practices, and local food systems helped to create new markets for farmers and improve food security for consumers. By the end of Harris's first term, the United States had made significant progress in reducing the environmental impact of agriculture, improving soil health, and supporting the livelihoods of farmers and ranchers.

The success of these new industries and the broader focus on sustainability demonstrated the potential of the "Build Back Better" plan to create a more dynamic and resilient economy. The investments in green jobs, infrastructure, and innovation not only helped to drive the economic recovery but also positioned the United States as a global leader in the 21st century economy.

The economic recovery and innovation efforts of the Harris administration were a defining feature of her presidency. The "Build Back Better" plan was ambitious and comprehensive, focusing on green jobs, infrastructure investment, and technological innovation. While the plan faced significant challenges, particularly in the areas of inflation and budget deficits, it ultimately yielded tangible results, creating new industries, revitalizing existing ones, and fostering a more sustainable and resilient economy.

Under Harris's leadership, the United States made significant progress in transitioning to a green economy, with rapid growth in renewable energy, electric vehicles, and sustainable agriculture. The administration's investments in infrastructure and technological innovation also helped to position the United States as a global leader in emerging technologies and advanced manufacturing.

The success of the "Build Back Better" plan demonstrated the potential of bold and visionary economic policies to drive recovery, create jobs, and address long-term challenges such as climate change and inequality. As the nation continued to navigate the challenges of the 21st century, the foundations laid by the Harris administration's economic recovery and innovation efforts would play a critical role in shaping the future of the United States and the global economy.

Chapter 5: Healthcare Reform and Expansion

The Urgent Need for Healthcare Reform

When Kamala Harris took office as President, one of her top priorities was healthcare reform. The COVID-19 pandemic had laid bare the weaknesses in the American healthcare system, exposing disparities in access to care, the high costs of medical treatment, and the gaps in insurance coverage. Millions of Americans had lost their health insurance during the pandemic due to job losses, and many more struggled with medical bills and inadequate care. Harris knew that addressing these issues was not only a moral imperative but also essential for the nation's long-term well-being.

The Affordable Care Act (ACA), passed during the Obama administration, had made significant strides in expanding healthcare coverage, reducing the number of uninsured Americans, and implementing essential consumer protections. However, it had also faced numerous challenges, including relentless attacks from Republicans, legal battles, and attempts to dismantle key provisions. By the time Harris assumed office, the ACA remained intact but was in need of expansion and improvement to address the ongoing issues in the healthcare system.

Harris had long been an advocate for healthcare reform. As a Senator, she had co-sponsored the Medicare for All Act, which proposed a single-payer healthcare system. However, as President, she recognized that the political reality required a more pragmatic approach. Her administration's healthcare agenda focused on building upon the successes of the ACA while introducing new measures to expand coverage, reduce costs, and improve the quality of care. Central to this agenda was the introduction of a public option, a government-run health insurance plan that would compete with private insurers.

Expanding the Affordable Care Act

The Harris administration's first step in healthcare reform was to expand the Affordable Care Act. Harris believed that the ACA had been a critical step forward in improving access to healthcare, but she also recognized that it needed to be strengthened and expanded to reach more Americans. The administration proposed a series of reforms aimed at increasing enrollment, enhancing benefits, and making healthcare more affordable.

One of the key components of the ACA expansion was increasing the subsidies available to individuals and families purchasing insurance through the health insurance marketplaces. Harris recognized that while the ACA had made coverage more accessible, many Americans still found the premiums and out-of-pocket costs too high. The administration's plan increased the size of the subsidies, extended them to more middle-income families, and capped the percentage of income that individuals had to pay for premiums.

In addition to expanding subsidies, the administration also focused on closing the Medicaid coverage gap. Under the ACA, states were given the option to expand Medicaid to cover all low-income adults up to 138% of the federal poverty level, with the federal government covering most of the cost. However, a significant number of states, primarily led by Republican governors and legislatures, had refused to expand Medicaid, leaving millions of low-income Americans without coverage.

To address this issue, Harris proposed a federal fallback option that would allow individuals in non-expansion states to enroll in a federally-administered Medicaid-like plan. This plan, known as the Medicaid Reserve, would provide comprehensive coverage to those who were eligible but lived in states that had not expanded Medicaid. The Medicaid Reserve would be funded entirely by the federal government, ensuring that no state could deny access to coverage for its residents.

The administration also sought to strengthen the ACA's consumer protections. This included reinstating the individual mandate, which required Americans to have health insurance or pay a penalty. The individual mandate had been repealed by the previous administration, leading to concerns that healthier individuals would opt out of coverage, driving up costs for everyone else. Harris believed that reinstating the mandate was essential to maintaining a stable insurance market and keeping premiums affordable.

Another critical reform was the expansion of essential health benefits (EHBs) required to be covered by all ACA-compliant plans. The administration proposed adding new benefits, such as coverage for mental health services, substance abuse treatment, and long-term care, recognizing the growing need for these services in the wake of the pandemic. The administration also worked to ensure that these benefits were robustly enforced, preventing insurers from offering plans with inadequate coverage.

Introducing the Public Option

One of the most significant and ambitious components of Harris's healthcare agenda was the introduction of a public option. The public option had been a major point of debate during the passage of the ACA, but it had ultimately been left out of the final legislation due to political opposition. Harris believed that the time was right to reintroduce the public option as a way to expand coverage, increase competition, and drive down costs.

The public option was designed as a government-run health insurance plan that would be available to all Americans, regardless of income or employment status. It would be offered alongside private plans on the ACA's health insurance marketplaces, providing consumers with a new choice in coverage. The public option would be funded by premiums and federal subsidies, but it would not be tied to employers, allowing individuals to maintain their coverage even if they changed jobs or became unemployed.

Harris envisioned the public option as a way to address some of the key shortcomings of the current healthcare system. First, it would provide an affordable alternative to private insurance, particularly in areas where there was little competition among insurers. The administration expected that the public option would be able to negotiate lower prices with healthcare providers and pharmaceutical companies, leading to lower premiums and out-of-pocket costs for enrollees.

Second, the public option would serve as a safety net for individuals who lost their employer-sponsored insurance or who were not eligible for Medicaid or other government programs. The plan would cover a comprehensive set of benefits, including preventive care, prescription drugs, mental health services, and maternity care, ensuring that all Americans had access to high-quality, affordable healthcare.

Third, the public option was intended to create downward pressure on healthcare costs by increasing competition in the insurance market. Harris believed that the presence of a government-run plan would force private insurers to lower their prices and improve their services to remain competitive. This, in turn, would benefit consumers by reducing premiums and out-of-pocket costs across the board.

The introduction of the public option was a major policy initiative, and it required significant planning and coordination across multiple agencies. The administration established a Public Option Task Force, chaired by Health and Human Services (HHS) Secretary Xavier Becerra, to oversee the design and implementation of the plan. The task force included representatives from the Centers for Medicare and Medicaid Services (CMS), the Department of the Treasury, and the Office of Management and Budget (OMB), as well as external experts in healthcare policy and administration.

The task force's first priority was to determine the structure of the public option, including how it would be funded, how premiums would be set, and how it would interact with existing programs like Medicare and Medicaid. The administration decided that the public option would be modeled after Medicare, with a network of providers and reimbursement rates similar to those used by the Medicare program. This approach was chosen because Medicare was already a well-established and popular program, and it provided a model for delivering high-quality care at lower costs.

The administration also worked to ensure that the public option would be available in all states, regardless of whether they had expanded Medicaid or participated fully in the ACA's marketplaces. This was a critical feature of the plan, as Harris was determined to ensure that all Americans had access to affordable coverage, no matter where they lived.

The Battles in Congress

While the public option was a central piece of Harris's healthcare agenda, it quickly became the focal point of intense political battles in Congress. Healthcare reform had long been one of the most contentious issues in American politics, and the introduction of a public option reignited many of the same debates that had surrounded the passage of the ACA.

The administration faced opposition from multiple fronts. On the right, Republicans were nearly unanimous in their opposition to the public option, viewing it as a step toward socialized medicine. They argued that a government-run plan would crowd out private insurers, lead to higher taxes, and ultimately result in lower quality care. Many Republican lawmakers were also concerned about the cost of the public option and its impact on the federal budget.

On the left, progressives were generally supportive of the public option but argued that it did not go far enough. Many progressives continued to advocate for a single-payer system, such as Medicare for All, which would eliminate private insurance altogether and provide universal coverage through a government-run program. While Harris had been a supporter of Medicare for All as a Senator, she recognized that it was not politically feasible in the current environment and that the public option was a more achievable goal.

In the center, moderate Democrats were divided on the issue. Some were concerned about the cost of the public option and its potential impact on the private insurance market, while others feared that supporting the public option would alienate voters in swing districts. These moderates were crucial to passing any healthcare legislation, and their support would be essential to getting the public option through Congress.

The administration launched an extensive campaign to build support for the public option, both within Congress and among the public. Harris and Vice President Tim Walz engaged in direct outreach to key lawmakers, meeting with moderate Democrats and Republicans to address their concerns and build consensus. The administration also worked with outside advocacy groups, including labor unions, consumer organizations, and healthcare advocates, to mobilize grassroots support for the plan.

Despite these efforts, the administration faced significant resistance from powerful healthcare lobbyists, including those representing private insurers, pharmaceutical companies, and hospital associations. These groups had long opposed the public option, fearing that it would cut into their profits and reduce their market share. They launched a well-funded campaign to block the public option, running ads, lobbying lawmakers, and mobilizing their networks to oppose the plan.

The debate over the public option reached a fever pitch in the Senate, where the administration needed to secure the support of all 50 Democratic senators, as well as the tie-breaking vote of Vice President Walz, to pass the legislation. The Senate was deeply divided, with several moderate Democrats expressing concerns about the cost and structure of the public option. Harris and her team worked tirelessly to address these concerns, offering concessions and adjustments to the plan to gain the necessary votes.

One of the key compromises was the inclusion of a state opt-out provision, which allowed states to choose not to participate in the public option if they could demonstrate that they had an alternative plan that provided comparable coverage at similar costs. This provision was intended to address concerns from moderate Democrats in states with strong private insurance markets, while still ensuring that the public option would be available in the majority of states.

Another compromise involved the reimbursement rates for providers participating in the public option. While the administration initially proposed using Medicare rates, which are lower than those paid by private insurers, this proposal faced pushback from hospital associations and some lawmakers who argued that it would lead to underpayment for healthcare services. The final compromise allowed for slightly higher reimbursement rates, closer to those used by private insurers, while still maintaining cost savings compared to traditional private plans.

Despite these concessions, the battle over the public option remained fierce. Republicans in the Senate were united in their opposition, and several moderate Democrats remained on the fence. The administration intensified its outreach efforts, with Harris personally meeting with holdout senators and making the case for the public option as a critical component of healthcare reform.

The turning point came when Senator Joe Manchin, a key moderate Democrat from West Virginia, announced his support for the public option, citing the need to provide affordable coverage to his constituents, many of whom were struggling with high healthcare costs. Manchin's support gave the administration the 50 votes it needed to pass the legislation, with Vice President Walz casting the tie-breaking vote in favor of the public option.

The passage of the public option in the Senate was a major victory for the Harris administration, but the battle was far from over. The legislation still needed to pass the House of Representatives, where it faced additional challenges from both progressives and moderates. The administration worked closely with House Speaker Hakeem Jeffries to navigate the legislative process, making further adjustments to the bill to secure the necessary votes.

In the end, the public option passed the House by a narrow margin, with strong support from progressives and enough moderate Democrats to offset the opposition from Republicans and some conservative Democrats. The passage of the public option was hailed as a major achievement for the Harris administration and a significant step forward in healthcare reform.

The Impact on American Families and the Healthcare Industry

The introduction of the public option and the expansion of the ACA had a profound impact on American families and the healthcare industry. For millions of Americans, the reforms meant access to affordable, comprehensive healthcare coverage for the first time. The public option provided a new choice in the insurance market, offering a high-quality, low-cost alternative to private plans.

One of the most immediate impacts of the public option was the reduction in the number of uninsured Americans. Within the first year of its implementation, millions of individuals and families who had previously been unable to afford coverage enrolled in the public option. This included many low-income Americans who had fallen into the Medicaid coverage gap, as well as those who had lost their employer-sponsored insurance during the pandemic.

The public option also had a positive impact on healthcare costs. The government-run plan was able to negotiate lower prices for healthcare services and prescription drugs, leading to lower premiums and out-of-pocket costs for enrollees. This, in turn, put pressure on private insurers to lower their prices to remain competitive, benefiting consumers across the board.

For American families, the expansion of the ACA and the introduction of the public option meant greater financial security and peace of mind. Many families who had previously been burdened by high medical bills and inadequate coverage were now able to access the care they needed without fear of financial ruin. The reforms also provided greater continuity of coverage, allowing individuals to maintain their insurance even if they changed jobs or experienced other life changes.

The impact of the reforms was particularly significant for communities of color and low-income populations, who had historically faced greater barriers to accessing healthcare. The expansion of Medicaid, the increased subsidies for marketplace plans, and the introduction of the public option all contributed to reducing racial and economic disparities in healthcare access and outcomes.

However, the reforms also had a significant impact on the healthcare industry, particularly on private insurers and pharmaceutical companies. The public option introduced new competition into the insurance market, forcing private insurers to lower their prices and improve their services. Some insurers struggled to compete with the government-run plan, leading to consolidation in the industry as smaller companies merged or exited the market.

The pharmaceutical industry also faced new challenges as the public option used its purchasing power to negotiate lower prices for prescription drugs. The administration's efforts to rein in drug costs were met with resistance from the industry, which argued that lower prices would stifle innovation and reduce investment in new treatments. However, Harris and her team countered that the reforms were necessary to make life-saving medications more affordable for all Americans.

Despite these challenges, the healthcare industry as a whole adapted to the new landscape. Hospitals and healthcare providers adjusted to the changes in reimbursement rates and coverage options, while private insurers found new ways to compete in the marketplace. The administration also worked to ensure that the public option and other reforms were implemented in a way that minimized disruption to the industry while maximizing benefits for consumers.

The healthcare reforms implemented by the Harris administration represented a significant step forward in the ongoing effort to improve access to affordable, high-quality healthcare in the United States. The expansion of the Affordable Care Act and the introduction of a public option provided new coverage options for millions of Americans, reduced healthcare costs, and addressed long-standing disparities in access and outcomes.

The battles in Congress and the resistance from powerful healthcare lobbyists highlighted the challenges of enacting meaningful healthcare reform in a deeply polarized political environment. However, the administration's persistence and willingness to compromise ultimately led to the passage of landmark legislation that had a profound impact on American families and the healthcare industry.

The reforms achieved under Harris's leadership demonstrated the potential of government action to address complex and entrenched problems in the healthcare system. While challenges remained, the expansion of the ACA and the introduction of the public option were important steps toward achieving the goal of universal healthcare coverage in the United States. As the nation continued to grapple with the evolving needs of its healthcare system, the reforms implemented by the Harris administration would serve as a foundation for future progress in the pursuit of a more just and equitable healthcare system.

Chapter 6: Racial Justice and Civil Rights

A Nation at a Crossroads

As Kamala Harris took the oath of office as the 47th President of the United States, the nation was at a pivotal moment in its history. The country was grappling with deep and persistent racial inequalities that had been laid bare in recent years, particularly in the aftermath of the high-profile killings of George Floyd, Breonna Taylor, and other Black Americans at the hands of law enforcement. These incidents had ignited a nationwide movement for racial justice, leading to protests in cities and towns across the country, and forcing a long-overdue reckoning with America's legacy of racism.

President Harris, as the first Black and South Asian woman to hold the office, understood the significance of this moment. Her own life story was deeply intertwined with the struggles for civil rights and equality. Her mother, an Indian immigrant and civil rights activist, had instilled in her the importance of fighting for justice and standing up against discrimination. Throughout her career, Harris had been a vocal advocate for civil rights, criminal justice reform, and racial equity. Now, as President, she was determined to lead the nation in addressing the systemic racism that had plagued it for centuries.

The Harris administration's racial justice agenda was ambitious and comprehensive, focusing on key areas such as police reform, criminal justice overhauls, economic equity, and the protection of civil rights.

Police Reform: A New Approach to Public Safety

One of the central pillars of the Harris administration's racial justice agenda was police reform. The killings of George Floyd, Breonna Taylor, and countless other Black Americans had sparked widespread outrage and underscored the urgent need for change in policing practices. The Harris administration recognized that reforming the nation's law enforcement agencies was essential to restoring trust between the police and the communities they served, particularly communities of color.

The administration's approach to police reform was multifaceted, addressing issues such as use of force, accountability, training, and community engagement. Harris believed that meaningful reform required both federal action and cooperation with state and local governments, as well as input from community leaders, civil rights organizations, and law enforcement professionals.

The George Floyd Justice in Policing Act 2.0

Early in her presidency, Harris introduced the George Floyd Justice in Policing Act 2.0, an updated and expanded version of the bill that had been introduced during the previous administration but had failed to pass the Senate. The new version of the bill aimed to address the concerns raised during the previous legislative debates while maintaining the core principles of accountability, transparency, and justice.

The George Floyd Justice in Policing Act 2.0 included several key provisions designed to curb police misconduct and enhance accountability:

1. Banning Chokeholds and No-Knock Warrants: The bill included a federal ban on chokeholds and carotid holds, as well as restrictions on the use of no-knock warrants in drug cases. These measures were in direct response to the circumstances surrounding the deaths of George Floyd and Breonna Taylor, and were intended to prevent similar tragedies in the future.

2. Ending Qualified Immunity: One of the most controversial aspects of the bill was its proposal to end qualified immunity for law enforcement officers. Qualified immunity had long shielded officers from civil lawsuits for actions taken in the line of duty, even in cases of clear misconduct. The bill sought to hold officers accountable by allowing victims of police violence to seek redress in court.

3. National Police Misconduct Registry: The bill established a national registry to track police misconduct and disciplinary actions. This registry was designed to prevent officers with a history of misconduct from moving between departments without accountability. It also required law enforcement agencies to report data on use of force, traffic stops, and other interactions with the public, disaggregated by race, gender, and other demographic factors.

4. Independent Investigations: The bill mandated that cases involving police use of deadly force be investigated by independent prosecutors or agencies, rather than by local law enforcement. This provision aimed to eliminate conflicts of interest and ensure impartial investigations.

5. Training and Community Policing: The bill provided federal funding for training programs focused on de-escalation, bias awareness, and crisis intervention. It also incentivized the adoption of community policing models that emphasized building relationships between officers and the communities they served.

The George Floyd Justice in Policing Act 2.0 was met with strong support from civil rights organizations, community leaders, and progressive lawmakers. However, it also faced significant opposition, particularly from police unions and conservative lawmakers who argued that the bill went too far and would undermine law enforcement's ability to do its job effectively.

The administration launched an extensive campaign to build support for the bill, engaging with stakeholders from all sides of the debate. Harris personally met with the families of victims of police violence, law enforcement officials, and members of Congress to discuss the importance of the legislation and to address concerns.

The bill faced a tough battle in Congress, particularly in the Senate, where Republicans and some moderate Democrats expressed reservations about certain provisions, particularly the ending of qualified immunity. Harris and her team worked tirelessly to build a coalition of support, offering amendments and compromises to address lawmakers' concerns without compromising the core principles of the bill.

In the end, the George Floyd Justice in Policing Act 2.0 passed both the House and the Senate by narrow margins, with Vice President Tim Walz casting the tie-breaking vote in the Senate. The passage of the bill was a significant victory for the Harris administration and a major step forward in the fight for racial justice and police reform.

Criminal Justice Overhaul: Addressing Systemic Injustices

Beyond police reform, the Harris administration also prioritized a comprehensive overhaul of the criminal justice system. Harris had long been a vocal advocate for criminal justice reform, having worked on issues such as reducing mass incarceration, eliminating cash bail, and addressing racial disparities in sentencing during her time as California's Attorney General and as a U.S. Senator.

The administration's criminal justice agenda was guided by the principles of fairness, accountability, and rehabilitation. Harris believed that the criminal justice system needed to be reimagined to prioritize prevention, treatment, and reentry, rather than punishment and incarceration.

The Sentencing Reform and Corrections Act

One of the centerpiece initiatives of the administration's criminal justice reform efforts was the Sentencing Reform and Corrections Act. This legislation aimed to address the disparities and injustices that had plagued the criminal justice system for decades, particularly those affecting communities of color.

The Sentencing Reform and Corrections Act included several key provisions:

1. Reducing Mandatory Minimum Sentences: The bill sought to reduce or eliminate mandatory minimum sentences for nonviolent drug offenses, which had been a major driver of mass incarceration, particularly for Black and Latino individuals. The bill also allowed for the retroactive application of reduced sentences, giving those currently serving long sentences for nonviolent offenses the opportunity for early release. Once marijuana was legalized nationwide during Harris' second term, this had the effect of emptying prisons, causing some for-profit institutions to close.

2. Expanding Alternatives to Incarceration: The bill promoted the use of alternatives to incarceration, such as diversion programs, drug courts, and community supervision, particularly for nonviolent offenders. These programs were designed to address the underlying causes of criminal behavior, such as substance abuse and mental health issues, while reducing the burden on the prison system.

3. Reforming Pretrial Practices: The bill included provisions to eliminate cash bail for most nonviolent offenses, recognizing that cash bail disproportionately affected low-income individuals and led to unnecessary pretrial detention. The bill also expanded the use of risk assessment tools to determine whether individuals could be safely released pending trial.

4. Addressing Racial Disparities: The bill required the Department of Justice (DOJ) to collect and report data on racial disparities in sentencing, incarceration, and other aspects of the criminal justice system. It also mandated that federal prosecutors receive training on implicit bias and the impact of racial disparities in the criminal justice system.

5. Supporting Reentry and Rehabilitation: The bill included funding for reentry programs that provided education, job training, and mental health services to individuals returning to society after incarceration. The goal was to reduce recidivism and support successful reintegration into the community.

The Sentencing Reform and Corrections Act received broad support from criminal justice reform advocates, civil rights organizations, and progressive lawmakers. However, it also faced significant opposition from some lawmakers, particularly those who believed that reducing sentences and expanding alternatives to incarceration would lead to increased crime rates.

The administration worked to build a bipartisan coalition in support of the bill, emphasizing the need for a more just and effective criminal justice system. Harris also highlighted the cost savings associated with reducing incarceration rates and investing in prevention and rehabilitation, arguing that these measures would ultimately lead to safer communities.

The Sentencing Reform and Corrections Act passed both the House and the Senate with bipartisan support, marking a major victory for the Harris administration and a significant step forward in the effort to address systemic injustices in the criminal justice system.

Economic Equity: Closing the Racial Wealth Gap

In addition to police reform and criminal justice overhaul, the Harris administration also focused on addressing the economic inequalities that had long plagued communities of color. The racial wealth gap—the disparity in wealth between White Americans and Black, Latino, and Indigenous Americans—was one of the most glaring examples of systemic racism in the United States.

Harris believed that addressing the racial wealth gap was essential to achieving true racial justice and that the federal government had a responsibility to take action. The administration's economic equity agenda included a range of initiatives aimed at closing the wealth gap, expanding opportunities for economic advancement, and supporting minority-owned businesses.

The Economic Equity Initiative

MADAM PRESIDENT: THE FIRST TERM OF KAMALA HARRIS

The Economic Equity Initiative was a comprehensive plan designed to address the structural barriers that had prevented communities of color from achieving economic prosperity. The initiative focused on several key areas:

1. Expanding Access to Capital: The initiative provided funding and support for minority-owned businesses, including grants, low-interest loans, and technical assistance. The administration also worked to increase access to capital for businesses in underserved communities, particularly those that had been disproportionately affected by the COVID-19 pandemic.

2. Promoting Homeownership: The initiative included measures to increase homeownership among Black and Latino families, who had historically faced discrimination in the housing market. This included expanding access to down payment assistance, increasing funding for affordable housing programs, and strengthening enforcement of fair housing laws.

3. Investing in Education and Workforce Development: The initiative provided funding for education and job training programs aimed at closing the skills gap and expanding opportunities for economic advancement. This included investments in Historically Black Colleges and Universities (HBCUs) and Minority-Serving Institutions (MSIs), as well as support for apprenticeships and vocational training programs.

4. Addressing Student Loan Debt: The initiative included measures to reduce the burden of student loan debt, which disproportionately affected Black and Latino students. This included expanding income-driven repayment plans, increasing funding for Pell Grants, and providing loan forgiveness for borrowers working in public service or underserved communities.

5. Strengthening Retirement Security: The initiative included measures to increase retirement security for workers of color, who were less likely to have access to employer-sponsored retirement plans. This included expanding access to retirement savings accounts, increasing funding for Social Security, and providing financial education and planning services.

The Economic Equity Initiative was met with strong support from civil rights organizations, community leaders, and progressive lawmakers. However, it also faced opposition from some conservative lawmakers who argued that the initiative was too costly and that it represented an overreach of federal government power.

The administration worked to build support for the initiative by highlighting the long-term benefits of closing the racial wealth gap, not only for communities of color but for the economy as a whole. Harris also emphasized the moral imperative of addressing the legacy of discrimination and ensuring that all Americans had the opportunity to achieve economic prosperity.

The Economic Equity Initiative was passed as part of the broader Build Back Better agenda, marking a significant step forward in the effort to address economic inequalities and close the racial wealth gap.

The Establishment of a New Civil Rights Commission

In addition to the specific policy initiatives focused on racial justice, the Harris administration also took steps to strengthen the federal government's ability to enforce civil rights laws and protect the rights of all Americans. One of the key components of this effort was the establishment of a new Civil Rights Commission, tasked with monitoring and enforcing civil rights legislation across the country.

The Civil Rights Commission: A Renewed Commitment to Justice

The Civil Rights Commission was established through an executive order signed by President Harris in her first year in office. The commission was designed to be an independent agency with the authority to investigate and address civil rights violations, monitor compliance with civil rights laws, and provide recommendations to Congress and the administration on how to strengthen civil rights protections.

The commission was composed of a diverse group of experts in civil rights law, policy, and advocacy, including representatives from civil rights organizations, academia, and government agencies. The commission was chaired by a prominent civil rights attorney, who had a long history of fighting for justice and equality.

The commission's mandate included several key responsibilities:

1. Investigating Civil Rights Violations: The commission was empowered to investigate allegations of civil rights violations, including discrimination in housing, employment, education, and voting rights. The commission had the authority to subpoena documents and testimony, conduct public hearings, and issue reports on its findings.

2. Monitoring Compliance with Civil Rights Laws: The commission was tasked with monitoring compliance with federal civil rights laws, including the Civil Rights Act, the Voting Rights Act, and the Fair Housing Act. This included reviewing the actions of federal agencies, state and local governments, and private entities to ensure that they were upholding civil rights protections.

3. Providing Recommendations: The commission was responsible for providing recommendations to Congress and the administration on how to strengthen civil rights protections and address emerging civil rights issues. This included recommendations for new legislation, regulatory changes, and enforcement actions.

4. Engaging with Communities: The commission was tasked with engaging with communities across the country to hear their concerns and gather input on civil rights issues. This included holding public hearings, town halls, and listening sessions in communities that had been affected by civil rights violations.

MADAM PRESIDENT: THE FIRST TERM OF KAMALA HARRIS

The establishment of the Civil Rights Commission was met with widespread praise from civil rights organizations, community leaders, and legal experts. Many saw the commission as a renewed commitment to the protection and advancement of civil rights in the United States, particularly at a time when many civil rights protections were under threat.

The commission quickly got to work, launching investigations into a range of civil rights issues, including voter suppression, housing discrimination, and police misconduct. The commission's reports and recommendations provided valuable insights into the state of civil rights in the United States and helped to inform the administration's policy decisions.

Key Moments of Tension and Breakthrough During Nationwide Protests

Throughout Harris's presidency, the nation continued to grapple with tensions over racial justice, leading to a number of key moments of tension and breakthrough. Nationwide protests, sparked by incidents of police violence and other civil rights violations, highlighted the ongoing struggle for justice and equality.

The Summer of 2025: Protests and Calls for Action

One of the most significant periods of tension occurred during the summer of 2025, when a series of high-profile incidents of police violence led to renewed protests in cities across the country. These protests, which were largely peaceful, drew attention to the ongoing issues of racial injustice and the need for further reform.

In one particularly high-profile case, the killing of a young Black man by police officers in a Southern city sparked outrage and led to weeks of protests. The incident was captured on video, showing the officers using excessive force against the unarmed man. The footage quickly went viral, leading to widespread condemnation and calls for justice.

The protests that followed were some of the largest since the summer of 2020, with demonstrators calling for accountability for the officers involved, as well as broader reforms to the criminal justice system. The protests were met with a heavy police presence, and there were several instances of clashes between protesters and law enforcement.

President Harris responded to the protests by calling for calm and urging both protesters and law enforcement to refrain from violence. She also reiterated her administration's commitment to police reform and criminal justice overhaul, emphasizing the need for accountability and justice.

Harris met with the family of the young man who had been killed, offering her condolences and pledging to do everything in her power to ensure that justice was served. She also announced that the Department of Justice would launch an investigation into the incident, as well as the broader practices of the police department involved.

The protests continued for several weeks, but they also led to important breakthroughs. In response to the public outcry, the city where the incident occurred agreed to implement a series of police reforms, including changes to use-of-force policies, increased oversight, and improved training for officers. The federal investigation also led to charges against the officers involved, who were later convicted of violating the young man's civil rights.

The summer of 2025 was a turning point in the fight for racial justice, demonstrating both the ongoing challenges and the potential for meaningful change. The protests highlighted the deep-seated issues that continued to plague the nation, but they also showed the power of collective action and the importance of holding those in power accountable.

Breakthrough: The Passage of the New Voting Rights Act

In the midst of the ongoing struggle for racial justice, the Harris administration achieved a major breakthrough with the passage of the New Voting Rights Act. The legislation was designed to restore and strengthen the protections of the original Voting Rights Act of 1965, which had been significantly weakened by a 2013 Supreme Court decision.

The New Voting Rights Act included several key provisions:

1. **Restoring Preclearance:** The bill restored the preclearance requirement, which mandated that states with a history of voter suppression receive federal approval before making changes to their voting laws. The bill also updated

the formula used to determine which states were subject to preclearance, ensuring that it reflected current conditions.

2. Protecting Voter Access: The bill included provisions to protect voter access, including measures to expand early voting, increase access to mail-in voting, and prevent voter ID laws that disproportionately affected communities of color.

3. Combating Voter Suppression: The bill strengthened the federal government's ability to combat voter suppression, including by increasing penalties for those who engaged in voter intimidation or other forms of voter suppression. It also provided funding for voter education and outreach efforts in communities that had been historically disenfranchised.

4. Promoting Election Security: The bill included measures to promote election security, including requirements for paper ballots, audits of election results, and increased funding for cybersecurity.

The passage of the New Voting Rights Act was a major victory for the Harris administration and a significant step forward in the fight to protect the right to vote. The legislation was passed with bipartisan support, reflecting a growing recognition of the importance of protecting the integrity of the electoral process.

The New Voting Rights Act was met with widespread praise from civil rights organizations, voting rights advocates, and community leaders. Many saw the legislation as a critical step toward ensuring that all Americans had the right to participate in the democratic process, regardless of race, income, or background.

The Harris administration's efforts to address racial justice and civil rights were among the most significant and challenging initiatives of her presidency. From police reform and criminal justice overhaul to economic equity and the protection of voting rights, the administration took bold steps to confront the systemic racism that had long plagued the nation.

The establishment of the Civil Rights Commission provided a renewed commitment to the protection and advancement of civil rights, while the administration's legislative achievements, including the George Floyd Justice in Policing Act 2.0 and the New Voting Rights Act, marked important milestones in the ongoing struggle for justice and equality.

Throughout her presidency, Harris navigated a landscape of tension and resistance, but she remained steadfast in her commitment to racial justice. The nationwide protests and calls for action that occurred during her time in office underscored the urgency of the issues at hand, but they also demonstrated the power of collective action and the potential for meaningful change.

As the nation continued to grapple with the challenges of racial inequality, the reforms and initiatives implemented by the Harris administration laid the foundation for a more just and equitable future. The progress achieved during her presidency was a testament to the enduring fight for civil rights and the belief that America could, and must, live up to its ideals of justice, equality, and freedom for all.

Chapter 7: Climate Change and Environmental Leadership

The Climate Crisis: A Defining Challenge

When Kamala Harris took office as President of the United States, the world was facing an existential threat that transcended national borders, political ideologies, and economic systems: climate change. The effects of global warming were already being felt around the world, with rising sea levels, more frequent and severe natural disasters, and shifting weather patterns that disrupted ecosystems and economies alike. Scientists warned that without immediate and decisive action, the planet would face catastrophic consequences, from widespread environmental degradation to mass displacement and economic collapse.

Harris recognized that addressing climate change was not only a moral imperative but also a defining challenge of her presidency. She believed that the United States, as one of the world's largest economies and a leading emitter of greenhouse gases, had a responsibility to lead the global fight against climate change. At the same time, she saw the climate crisis as an opportunity to transform the U.S. economy, create millions of green jobs, and position the country as a leader in the emerging clean energy sector.

Rejoining the Paris Agreement: A Renewed Commitment to Global Climate Action

One of Kamala Harris's first actions as President was to rejoin the Paris Agreement, the landmark international accord aimed at combating climate change by limiting global warming to well below 2 degrees Celsius above pre-industrial levels. The previous administration had withdrawn the United States from the agreement, citing concerns about its impact on the U.S. economy and questioning the science behind climate change. This decision had drawn widespread condemnation from the international community and environmental advocates, who saw it as a retreat from global leadership on one of the most pressing issues of our time.

Harris's decision to rejoin the Paris Agreement sent a powerful message to the world: the United States was once again committed to leading the fight against climate change. In her announcement, Harris emphasized the urgency of the climate crisis and the need for global cooperation to address it. She framed climate action not only as a necessity for the planet's future but also as an opportunity to drive economic growth, create jobs, and build a more sustainable and equitable world.

Rejoining the Paris Agreement was just the first step. Harris understood that the U.S. needed to do more than simply recommit to the goals of the agreement; it needed to set an example by taking bold and ambitious action to reduce greenhouse gas emissions and transition to a clean energy economy. To that end, she announced a series of aggressive climate targets for the United States, including:

MADAM PRESIDENT: THE FIRST TERM OF KAMALA HARRIS

1. Net-Zero Emissions by 2050: Harris set a goal of achieving net-zero greenhouse gas emissions by 2050, with an interim target of reducing emissions by 50% from 2005 levels by 2030. This would require a massive transformation of the U.S. energy sector, as well as significant changes in transportation, agriculture, and other key industries.

2. 100% Clean Electricity by 2035: Harris committed to transitioning the U.S. electricity grid to 100% clean, renewable energy by 2035. This goal was designed to accelerate the deployment of wind, solar, and other renewable energy sources, while phasing out fossil fuels and reducing reliance on natural gas.

3. Phasing Out Fossil Fuel Subsidies: Harris pledged to eliminate federal subsidies for fossil fuels, redirecting those funds toward clean energy research, development, and deployment. This policy aimed to level the playing field for renewable energy and encourage the private sector to invest in sustainable alternatives.

4. Investing in Climate Resilience: Recognizing that the impacts of climate change were already being felt across the country, Harris committed to investing in climate resilience and adaptation measures. This included funding for infrastructure upgrades, disaster preparedness, and community-based initiatives to protect vulnerable populations from the effects of climate change.

These climate goals were among the most ambitious ever set by a U.S. president, and they required a comprehensive and coordinated effort across the federal government, state and local governments, the private sector, and civil society. Harris's administration worked quickly to develop and implement policies that would put the country on track to meet these targets, while also engaging with international partners to strengthen global climate action.

The Green New Deal: Transforming the Energy Sector

Central to Harris's climate agenda was the Green New Deal, a bold and visionary framework for addressing the climate crisis while also tackling economic inequality and promoting social justice. The Green New Deal was first introduced in Congress in 2019 by Representative Alexandria Ocasio-Cortez (AOC) and Senator Ed Markey, and it quickly became a rallying cry for progressives and climate activists across the country.

The Green New Deal called for a sweeping transformation of the U.S. economy, with a focus on decarbonizing key sectors, creating millions of green jobs, and addressing the historical injustices that had disproportionately affected low-income communities and communities of color. The framework was inspired by the New Deal of the 1930s, which had helped lift the United States out of the Great Depression through massive public investment in infrastructure, social programs, and job creation.

Harris had been an early supporter of the Green New Deal, and as President, she made it a cornerstone of her climate policy. She recognized that achieving the ambitious climate goals she had set for the country would require the kind of transformative action envisioned by the Green New Deal. To that end, her administration worked closely with AOC and other key proponents of the Green New Deal to develop and implement a series of initiatives aimed at transforming the energy sector and driving the transition to a clean energy economy.

Investing in Renewable Energy

One of the key components of the Green New Deal was the rapid expansion of renewable energy, particularly wind and solar power. Harris's administration committed to investing hundreds of billions of dollars in the development and deployment of renewable energy technologies, with the goal of making clean energy the dominant source of power in the United States.

The administration's renewable energy strategy focused on several key areas:

1. Incentives for Renewable Energy Projects: The administration expanded tax credits and other incentives for renewable energy projects, making it more financially viable for companies and utilities to invest in wind, solar, and other clean energy sources. These incentives helped drive a surge in new renewable energy projects across the country, particularly in regions with high potential for wind and solar power.

2. Upgrading the Electricity Grid: The administration invested in modernizing the U.S. electricity grid to

accommodate the increased use of renewable energy. This included funding for the development of smart grid technologies, energy storage systems, and transmission infrastructure to connect renewable energy projects to the grid. These upgrades were essential for ensuring that the grid could handle the variability of renewable energy sources and provide reliable power to consumers.

3. Supporting Offshore Wind Development: The administration prioritized the development of offshore wind energy, particularly along the East Coast. Offshore wind had the potential to generate significant amounts of clean energy, and the administration provided funding and regulatory support to accelerate the permitting and construction of offshore wind farms.

4. Investing in Energy Efficiency: In addition to expanding renewable energy, the administration also focused on improving energy efficiency in buildings, transportation, and industry. The Green New Deal included funding for energy efficiency retrofits, incentives for energy-efficient appliances and vehicles, and support for research and development of new energy-saving technologies.

The investments in renewable energy and energy efficiency quickly began to pay off. By the end of Harris's first term, the United States had significantly increased its renewable energy capacity, with wind and solar power accounting for a growing share of the nation's electricity generation. The transition to clean energy also created millions of new jobs, particularly in construction, manufacturing, and engineering.

Phasing Out Fossil Fuels

Another key goal of the Green New Deal was to phase out the use of fossil fuels, which were the primary source of greenhouse gas emissions in the United States. Harris's administration took several steps to reduce the country's reliance on coal, oil, and natural gas, while supporting workers and communities affected by the transition.

1. Ending Fossil Fuel Subsidies: One of the administration's first actions was to eliminate federal subsidies for fossil fuels, which had long provided financial support to the coal, oil, and gas industries. By redirecting these funds toward clean energy, the administration aimed to level the playing field and encourage the private sector to invest in renewable energy.

2. Implementing a Carbon Price: The administration worked with Congress to pass legislation that established a carbon price, which required companies to pay for the carbon dioxide emissions they produced. The carbon price provided a financial incentive for companies to reduce their emissions and invest in cleaner alternatives. The revenue generated from the carbon price was used to fund climate resilience projects and support low-income households affected by the transition.

3. Supporting a Just Transition: Recognizing that the transition away from fossil fuels would have significant

economic impacts on workers and communities dependent on the coal, oil, and gas industries, the administration implemented a Just Transition Plan. This plan provided financial assistance, job training, and economic development support to workers and communities affected by the transition. The goal was to ensure that the benefits of the clean energy economy were shared broadly and that no one was left behind.

4. Strengthening Environmental Regulations: The administration also took steps to strengthen environmental regulations on fossil fuel extraction, transportation, and use. This included tighter controls on methane emissions from oil and gas operations, increased oversight of coal mining, and stricter standards for air and water pollution from fossil fuel power plants.

The administration's efforts to phase out fossil fuels faced significant opposition from the fossil fuel industry and its political allies. However, Harris was resolute in her commitment to addressing climate change and believed that the long-term benefits of the transition to clean energy far outweighed the short-term challenges.

International Climate Leadership: Reasserting U.S. Influence

In addition to her domestic climate agenda, Harris was also committed to reasserting U.S. leadership on the global stage. The previous administration's withdrawal from the Paris Agreement had damaged the United States' reputation as a global leader on climate issues, and Harris was determined to restore that leadership and build stronger international partnerships to address the climate crisis.

International Climate Summits

One of Harris's first major international actions as President was to convene a Global Climate Summit, bringing together world leaders, environmental organizations, and industry representatives to discuss the urgent need for coordinated global action on climate change. The summit was held in Washington, D.C., and was attended by leaders from more than 100 countries, as well as representatives from the United Nations, the European Union, and other international organizations.

At the summit, Harris announced the United States' renewed commitment to the Paris Agreement and its ambitious climate goals. She also called on other countries to strengthen their climate commitments and increase their contributions to global climate finance, particularly for developing countries that were most vulnerable to the impacts of climate change.

The Global Climate Summit resulted in several key agreements, including:

1. Strengthening Nationally Determined Contributions (NDCs): Harris urged all countries to submit new or updated NDCs, which are the national targets for reducing greenhouse gas emissions under the Paris Agreement. Many countries responded by announcing more ambitious targets,

with several committing to achieving net-zero emissions by mid-century.

2. Increasing Climate Finance: Harris announced that the United States would significantly increase its contributions to international climate finance, providing funding for climate mitigation and adaptation projects in developing countries. She also called on other developed countries to fulfill their financial commitments under the Paris Agreement and provide additional support to vulnerable nations.

3. Promoting Climate Resilience: The summit highlighted the need for greater investment in climate resilience and adaptation, particularly in regions that were already experiencing the impacts of climate change. The United States committed to providing technical assistance, capacity-building support, and funding for climate resilience projects in vulnerable countries.

4. Advancing Clean Energy Innovation: The summit also focused on the importance of clean energy innovation in achieving global climate goals. Harris announced the launch of the Clean Energy Innovation Partnership, a new international initiative aimed at accelerating the development and deployment of clean energy technologies. The partnership brought together governments, private sector companies, and research institutions to collaborate on clean energy research and share best practices.

MADAM PRESIDENT: THE FIRST TERM OF KAMALA HARRIS

The success of the Global Climate Summit helped to restore the United States' credibility as a leader on climate issues and laid the groundwork for stronger international cooperation. Harris's leadership at the summit was widely praised, and she emerged as a key figure in the global climate movement.

The U.S. as a Global Leader

Following the Global Climate Summit, Harris continued to assert U.S. leadership on climate issues through a series of high-profile international engagements. She attended the annual United Nations Climate Change Conference (COP), where she delivered a powerful speech calling for urgent global action to address the climate crisis.

At COP, Harris announced several new U.S. initiatives, including a pledge to achieve net-zero emissions from federal operations by 2040 and a commitment to phase out the use of hydrofluorocarbons (HFCs), a potent greenhouse gas used in refrigeration and air conditioning. She also called on other countries to join the United States in phasing out HFCs and adopting cleaner alternatives.

Harris's leadership on climate issues extended beyond the COP conferences. She played a key role in brokering a new international agreement to reduce methane emissions, which was signed by more than 100 countries. The agreement committed signatories to reducing methane emissions by 30% by 2030 and included provisions for monitoring, reporting, and verification of emissions reductions.

In addition to these international agreements, Harris also worked to strengthen bilateral climate partnerships with key countries, including China, the European Union, and India. These partnerships focused on areas such as clean energy development, climate finance, and technology transfer, with the goal of accelerating global progress toward the Paris Agreement's goals.

The Role of AOC and the Rise of the Green New Deal

Throughout Harris's presidency, one of her most important allies in the fight against climate change was Representative Alexandria Ocasio-Cortez (AOC). AOC had first gained national attention as one of the youngest women ever elected to Congress and as a vocal advocate for progressive policies, including the Green New Deal.

AOC's role in advancing the Green New Deal and pushing for bold climate action made her a key figure in the Harris administration's climate agenda. She worked closely with the administration to develop and promote key climate initiatives, and her leadership helped to galvanize public support for the Green New Deal and other climate policies.

AOC's influence extended beyond her role in Congress. She became a leading voice in the global climate movement, advocating for climate justice, economic equity, and the need for systemic change to address the root causes of the climate crisis. Her speeches and public appearances drew large crowds, and she used her platform to amplify the voices of marginalized communities and to call for urgent action on climate change.

In 2028, tragedy struck when Vice President Tim Walz passed away unexpectedly. His death was a significant loss for the administration and the country, as Walz had been a steady and reliable partner for Harris throughout her presidency. In the aftermath of his passing, Harris faced the difficult task of selecting a new Vice President.

After careful consideration, Harris chose AOC as her new Vice President. The decision was met with widespread praise from progressives and climate activists, who saw AOC as a natural choice given her leadership on climate issues and her close alignment with Harris's vision for the country.

AOC's appointment as Vice President marked a historic moment, as she became the youngest person ever to hold the office and the first Latina to do so. Her elevation to the role of Vice President also signaled a new era of progressive leadership in the United States, with a focus on addressing climate change, economic inequality, and social justice.

As Vice President, AOC continued to play a central role in the administration's climate agenda. She worked closely with Harris to advance key initiatives, including the implementation of the Green New Deal and the continued expansion of renewable energy. She also represented the United States at international climate conferences, where she advocated for stronger global action and the need to center climate justice in all climate policies.

Kamala Harris's leadership on climate change and environmental issues was one of the defining aspects of her presidency. From rejoining the Paris Agreement to setting ambitious climate goals, to implementing the Green New Deal, Harris positioned the United States as a global leader in the fight against climate change.

The transformation of the energy sector, driven by the Green New Deal and other climate initiatives, created millions of green jobs, reduced the country's reliance on fossil fuels, and put the United States on a path to a more sustainable and equitable future. Harris's commitment to international cooperation and her leadership at global climate summits helped to strengthen the global response to the climate crisis and ensured that the United States played a key role in shaping the future of the planet.

The appointment of Alexandria Ocasio-Cortez as Vice President following the tragic passing of Tim Walz further underscored the administration's commitment to bold climate action and progressive leadership. AOC's influence and leadership on climate issues, both domestically and internationally, helped to ensure that the United States remained at the forefront of the global fight against climate change.

As the world continued to grapple with the challenges of climate change, the leadership of Kamala Harris and AOC provided a beacon of hope and a model for how bold, visionary action could address one of the most pressing issues of our time. Their efforts laid the foundation for a more sustainable, just, and resilient world, ensuring that future generations would inherit a planet that was healthier, more equitable, and more secure.

Chapter 8: Foreign Policy Redefined

The Harris Doctrine: A New Era of American Diplomacy

When Kamala Harris was sworn in as the 47th President of the United States, the world was watching closely. The previous administration had left American foreign policy in disarray, marked by a retreat from international institutions, strained alliances, and an "America First" approach that had often isolated the United States on the global stage. As the first woman, first Black woman, and first person of South Asian descent to hold the office, Harris brought a fresh perspective to the presidency. Her foreign policy approach, soon dubbed the "Harris Doctrine," aimed to restore America's leadership through diplomacy, multilateralism, and a commitment to shared global challenges.

The Harris Doctrine was built on several core principles:

1. Diplomacy First: Harris emphasized the importance of diplomacy as the primary tool of American foreign policy. She believed that the United States should lead by example, using dialogue and negotiation to resolve conflicts, build alliances, and promote peace and security.

2. Multilateralism and International Cooperation: Harris was a staunch advocate of multilateralism, recognizing that

global challenges such as climate change, pandemics, and terrorism could only be effectively addressed through international cooperation. Under her leadership, the United States re-engaged with international institutions and worked to strengthen global governance.

3. Human Rights and Democracy: Harris placed a strong emphasis on human rights and the promotion of democratic values. She believed that the United States had a responsibility to support freedom and justice around the world, and her administration made human rights a central focus of its foreign policy.

4. Strategic Alliances: Harris recognized the importance of strong alliances in maintaining global stability and addressing shared challenges. She worked to rebuild and strengthen America's traditional alliances, particularly with NATO and other key partners, while also forging new partnerships in emerging regions.

5. Global Leadership in Addressing Transnational Challenges: The Harris Doctrine emphasized America's role as a global leader in addressing transnational challenges such as climate change, cybersecurity, and public health. Harris believed that the United States should take the lead in developing and implementing global solutions to these pressing issues.

As President, Harris faced a rapidly changing global landscape. The rise of China, the resurgence of Russia, ongoing conflicts in the Middle East, and the challenges of climate change and pandemics required a foreign policy that was both nimble and forward-looking. The Harris Doctrine was her answer to these challenges, providing a framework for re-establishing America's role on the world stage.

Re-Engaging with NATO and Rebuilding Alliances

One of the first priorities of the Harris administration was to rebuild and strengthen America's alliances, particularly with NATO. The previous administration had strained relations with many of America's traditional allies, questioning the value of NATO and criticizing member countries for not meeting their defense spending commitments. This had led to concerns about the future of the alliance and the United States' commitment to collective defense.

Harris understood that a strong NATO was essential for maintaining global stability and deterring aggression, particularly from Russia. Her administration moved quickly to reaffirm America's commitment to the alliance and to work with NATO members to address shared security challenges.

The Brussels Summit: Reaffirming the Transatlantic Alliance

In her first year in office, Harris attended the NATO Summit in Brussels, Belgium. The summit was a critical opportunity for her to reset relations with America's European allies and to reaffirm the United States' commitment to NATO.

MADAM PRESIDENT: THE FIRST TERM OF KAMALA HARRIS

In her address to the summit, Harris emphasized the importance of the transatlantic alliance and the shared values that underpinned it. She acknowledged the concerns of NATO members about the previous administration's rhetoric and reassured them that the United States was fully committed to the alliance.

"We stand together in defense of our shared values—democracy, freedom, and the rule of law," Harris said in her speech. "The United States is committed to our NATO allies, and we will work together to ensure that this alliance remains strong and capable of meeting the challenges of the 21st century."

Harris also used the summit to address concerns about defense spending. While reaffirming the United States' commitment to NATO's collective defense, she urged European allies to increase their defense budgets to meet the alliance's spending targets. However, she did so in a tone that emphasized cooperation rather than confrontation, recognizing the economic challenges that many countries faced in the wake of the COVID-19 pandemic.

The Brussels Summit marked a significant turning point in U.S.-NATO relations. Harris's emphasis on diplomacy, multilateralism, and shared values resonated with NATO members, and the summit concluded with a renewed commitment to the alliance. Harris also announced several new initiatives, including increased funding for NATO's cyber defense capabilities and a commitment to enhance the alliance's readiness to respond to emerging threats, such as hybrid warfare and disinformation campaigns.

The G7 Summit: Leading on Global Challenges

In addition to the NATO Summit, Harris also played a key role at the G7 Summit, which brought together leaders from the world's largest advanced economies to discuss global challenges. The summit, held in the United Kingdom, provided an opportunity for Harris to demonstrate America's leadership on issues such as climate change, global health, and economic recovery.

At the G7 Summit, Harris pushed for ambitious commitments on climate change, urging the world's leading economies to take stronger action to reduce greenhouse gas emissions and support the transition to clean energy. She also announced the United States' commitment to contribute significantly to the Green Climate Fund, which provides financial support to developing countries for climate mitigation and adaptation efforts.

Harris also focused on global health, calling for increased international cooperation to prevent and respond to future pandemics. She proposed the creation of a Global Health Security Initiative, which would bring together governments, international organizations, and the private sector to strengthen global health systems and improve pandemic preparedness. The initiative received broad support from G7 leaders, and a working group was established to develop a framework for its implementation.

The G7 Summit also provided an opportunity for Harris to engage with key allies on economic recovery efforts in the wake of the COVID-19 pandemic. Harris emphasized the importance of inclusive and sustainable growth, calling for increased investments in infrastructure, education, and innovation to drive economic recovery and reduce inequality. She also advocated for global tax reform, including the establishment of a minimum corporate tax rate to prevent tax avoidance by multinational corporations.

The G7 Summit was widely seen as a success, with Harris emerging as a key leader on global issues. Her emphasis on multilateralism, cooperation, and shared values helped to restore America's standing on the world stage and demonstrated the United States' commitment to addressing global challenges.

Engaging with China: Navigating a Complex Relationship

One of the most significant foreign policy challenges facing the Harris administration was managing the United States' relationship with China. As the world's second-largest economy and a rising global power, China presented both opportunities and challenges for the United States. Harris recognized that the U.S.-China relationship would be one of the most important and complex aspects of her foreign policy, requiring a careful balance of competition and cooperation.

The Beijing Dialogue: A New Approach to U.S.-China Relations

Early in her presidency, Harris initiated the Beijing Dialogue, a series of high-level talks between the United States and China aimed at addressing areas of mutual concern and exploring opportunities for cooperation. The dialogue was intended to reset the U.S.-China relationship after years of escalating tensions and to establish a framework for managing the complex and multifaceted relationship between the two countries.

The Beijing Dialogue covered a wide range of issues, including trade, cybersecurity, climate change, human rights, and regional security. Harris made it clear that the United States was committed to engaging with China on these issues, but she also emphasized the importance of standing firm on American values and interests.

One of the key areas of focus in the dialogue was trade. The previous administration's trade war with China had led to increased tariffs and economic uncertainty, affecting both countries and the global economy. Harris sought to de-escalate the trade tensions while also addressing concerns about China's trade practices, including intellectual property theft, market access, and state subsidies.

As part of the dialogue, Harris's administration negotiated a new trade agreement with China that aimed to address these issues while promoting fair and reciprocal trade. The agreement included provisions for stronger intellectual property protections, increased market access for U.S. companies, and commitments from China to reduce state subsidies for certain industries. In return, the United States agreed to reduce some of the tariffs imposed during the trade war, providing relief to American businesses and consumers.

While the trade agreement was a significant achievement, the Beijing Dialogue also addressed other critical issues in the U.S.-China relationship. On cybersecurity, the two countries agreed to establish a joint working group to address cyber threats and reduce the risk of cyber conflict. The working group was tasked with developing norms for responsible state behavior in cyberspace and enhancing cooperation on cybersecurity issues.

Climate change was another key area of focus in the dialogue. Harris recognized that addressing the global climate crisis required cooperation between the world's two largest emitters of greenhouse gases. As part of the dialogue, the United States and China agreed to enhance cooperation on clean energy development, emissions reduction, and climate resilience. The two countries also committed to working together to support global climate action, particularly in developing countries.

Human rights, however, remained a contentious issue in the U.S.-China relationship. Harris was a vocal critic of China's human rights record, particularly its treatment of ethnic minorities, including the Uyghurs in Xinjiang, and its crackdown on political freedoms in Hong Kong. While the Beijing Dialogue provided an opportunity for the United

States to raise these concerns directly with Chinese officials, it also highlighted the deep differences between the two countries on issues of governance and human rights.

The Beijing Dialogue was seen as a positive step toward managing the U.S.-China relationship, but it also underscored the complexity and challenges of dealing with a rising global power. Harris's approach to China was characterized by a commitment to engagement and diplomacy, balanced with a firm stance on American values and interests.

Navigating International Crises: Successes and Setbacks

The Harris administration faced numerous international crises during its time in office, each of which tested the principles of the Harris Doctrine and the administration's ability to navigate complex global challenges. While the administration achieved several notable successes, it also faced setbacks and challenges that underscored the difficulties of managing a rapidly changing global landscape.

The Middle East: Managing Conflict and Promoting Stability

One of the most significant challenges facing the Harris administration was managing the ongoing conflicts and instability in the Middle East. The region had long been a focal point of U.S. foreign policy, and Harris recognized the need for a new approach that emphasized diplomacy, conflict resolution, and support for regional stability.

The Iran Nuclear Deal: Reviving Diplomacy

One of Harris's top priorities in the Middle East was to revive the Iran nuclear deal, formally known as the Joint Comprehensive Plan of Action (JCPOA). The previous administration had withdrawn the United States from the JCPOA, leading to increased tensions between the United States and Iran and raising concerns about Iran's nuclear program.

Harris believed that diplomacy was the best path forward for addressing the Iranian nuclear issue and preventing further escalation in the region. Early in her presidency, she initiated diplomatic efforts to bring Iran back to the negotiating table and to rejoin the JCPOA.

The negotiations were complex and challenging, as both the United States and Iran had taken steps that complicated the path to an agreement. Iran had resumed uranium enrichment and other nuclear activities in response to the U.S. withdrawal from the JCPOA, while the United States had imposed new sanctions on Iran.

Despite these challenges, Harris's administration remained committed to diplomacy. After months of negotiations, the United States and Iran reached an agreement to return to full compliance with the JCPOA. Under the terms of the agreement, Iran agreed to roll back its nuclear activities in exchange for the lifting of U.S. sanctions.

The revival of the JCPOA was seen as a major diplomatic achievement for the Harris administration and a significant step toward reducing tensions in the Middle East. However, the agreement also faced criticism from some quarters, particularly from those who believed that it did not go far enough in addressing Iran's regional activities and its ballistic missile program.

The Israeli-Palestinian Conflict: Pursuing a Two-State Solution

The Israeli-Palestinian conflict was another major challenge facing the Harris administration. The conflict had persisted for decades, with numerous attempts at peace negotiations failing to produce a lasting resolution. Harris believed that the United States had a responsibility to play a leading role in pursuing a peaceful solution to the conflict.

Harris's approach to the Israeli-Palestinian conflict was grounded in her commitment to a two-state solution, which she believed was the only viable path to lasting peace. Early in her presidency, she appointed a special envoy for Middle East peace, tasked with reviving negotiations between Israel and the Palestinian Authority.

The special envoy worked to build trust between the parties and to address key issues such as borders, security, refugees, and the status of Jerusalem. Harris also emphasized the importance of economic development and support for Palestinian institutions as part of the peace process.

Despite these efforts, progress on the Israeli-Palestinian conflict was slow and difficult. The deep divisions between the parties, coupled with ongoing violence and settlement activity, made it challenging to move forward with negotiations. While Harris's administration was able to secure some modest agreements on economic cooperation and security coordination, a comprehensive peace agreement remained elusive.

The Israeli-Palestinian conflict highlighted the limitations of U.S. influence in a region marked by deep-seated divisions and longstanding grievances. While Harris remained committed to pursuing a two-state solution, she recognized that achieving lasting peace would require sustained diplomatic efforts and the support of the international community.

Successes and Setbacks: The Complex Realities of Foreign Policy

Throughout her presidency, Kamala Harris faced a complex and rapidly changing global landscape. Her foreign policy, defined by the Harris Doctrine, was grounded in diplomacy, multilateralism, and a commitment to shared global challenges. While the administration achieved several notable successes, it also faced significant setbacks and challenges that underscored the difficulties of managing international crises.

Successes: Rebuilding Alliances and Leading on Global Challenges

One of the key successes of the Harris administration's foreign policy was the rebuilding of America's alliances and the reassertion of U.S. leadership on the global stage. Harris's emphasis on diplomacy and multilateralism helped to restore trust and cooperation with key allies, particularly through NATO and the G7.

Harris's leadership on global challenges, such as climate change and global health, also earned the United States renewed respect and influence in international forums. The Global Climate Summit and the G7 Summit were both seen as major successes, demonstrating America's commitment to addressing pressing global issues and working with international partners to find solutions.

The administration's efforts to engage with China through the Beijing Dialogue also yielded positive results, with significant progress made on trade, cybersecurity, and climate cooperation. While the U.S.-China relationship remained complex and challenging, the dialogue provided a framework for managing competition and cooperation between the two countries.

Setbacks: Navigating International Crises

Despite these successes, the Harris administration also faced significant setbacks in navigating international crises. The withdrawal from Afghanistan was perhaps the most notable example, with the rapid collapse of the Afghan government and the chaotic evacuation process raising serious questions about the administration's handling of the situation.

The ongoing challenges in the Middle East, particularly the Israeli-Palestinian conflict and the struggle to address Iran's regional activities, also highlighted the limitations of U.S.

influence in a region marked by deep-seated divisions and longstanding conflicts.

These setbacks underscored the complexities of managing international crises and the difficulties of achieving lasting solutions in a rapidly changing global landscape. Harris's administration was forced to confront the realities of a world in which traditional power dynamics were shifting, and new challenges were emerging.

The Legacy of the Harris Doctrine

As Kamala Harris's presidency drew to a close, the legacy of her foreign policy—the Harris Doctrine—was still being written. Her emphasis on diplomacy, multilateralism, and global leadership had helped to restore America's standing on the world stage and to reassert the United States as a key player in addressing global challenges.

The successes of the Harris Doctrine were evident in the rebuilding of alliances, the progress made on climate change and global health, and the re-engagement with international institutions. Harris's leadership on these issues demonstrated the importance of cooperation, dialogue, and shared values in navigating a complex and rapidly changing world.

At the same time, the setbacks and challenges faced by the Harris administration highlighted the difficulties of managing international crises and the limitations of U.S. influence in certain regions. The withdrawal from Afghanistan, in particular, served as a reminder of the complexities and risks of ending protracted conflicts and the challenges of achieving lasting peace and stability.

Ultimately, the Harris Doctrine reflected a vision of American foreign policy that was grounded in the belief that the United States could lead by example, through diplomacy, cooperation, and a commitment to shared global challenges. As the world continued to grapple with the challenges of the 21st century, the principles of the Harris Doctrine would continue to shape America's role on the world stage and its relationships with allies, adversaries, and the global community.

Chapter 9: Immigration and Border Policy

A Nation of Immigrants: The Challenge of Reform

From the moment Kamala Harris announced her candidacy for the presidency, immigration reform was one of the defining issues of her campaign. The United States, a nation built by immigrants, had long struggled with how to manage immigration in a way that balanced the ideals of openness and inclusivity with concerns about security, economic impact, and social cohesion. Over the years, the issue had become increasingly polarizing, with deep divisions along political and ideological lines.

As President, Harris was committed to addressing the complexities of immigration in a way that honored America's history as a nation of immigrants while also ensuring that the immigration system was fair, orderly, and humane. Her administration's approach to immigration reform was guided by several key principles: providing a pathway to citizenship for undocumented immigrants, ensuring border security while treating migrants with dignity and respect, and addressing the root causes of migration from Central America and other regions.

The task of reforming immigration was immense and fraught with challenges. The U.S. immigration system was not only outdated but also overwhelmed by years of political gridlock and piecemeal reforms. The border, meanwhile, had become a flashpoint for both humanitarian crises and national security concerns, with large numbers of migrants arriving in search of safety and opportunity. Harris knew that meaningful reform would require both bold action and careful negotiation, as well as the ability to navigate a deeply divided Congress and a country grappling with the social and political implications of immigration.

A Pathway to Citizenship: Fulfilling the American Dream

One of the central pillars of the Harris administration's immigration policy was the creation of a pathway to citizenship for the millions of undocumented immigrants living in the United States. Harris believed that these individuals, many of whom had lived in the country for decades, contributed to the economy, enriched the culture, and deserved the opportunity to become full members of the society they had helped to build.

The American Dream Act

Early in her presidency, Harris introduced the American Dream Act, a comprehensive immigration reform bill designed to provide a pathway to citizenship for undocumented immigrants, while also addressing other key aspects of the immigration system. The bill was named in honor of the "American Dream," the idea that anyone, regardless of their background, could achieve success and prosperity through hard work and determination.

The American Dream Act included several key provisions:

1. Pathway to Citizenship: The bill provided a pathway to citizenship for undocumented immigrants who met certain criteria, including continuous residence in the United States, payment of back taxes, and a clean criminal record. Those who qualified would be eligible to apply for temporary legal status, which could later be converted to permanent residency and, ultimately, citizenship after a period of five years.

2. Protections for DREAMers: The bill codified the protections provided under the Deferred Action for Childhood Arrivals (DACA) program, ensuring that DREAMers—undocumented immigrants who were brought to the United States as children—could remain in the country without fear of deportation. It also provided a pathway to citizenship for DREAMers, recognizing that they were Americans in every way except for their legal status.

3. Family Reunification: The bill included provisions to expedite the reunification of families who had been separated by the immigration system. It prioritized visa processing for family members of U.S. citizens and legal residents, and it included measures to reduce the backlog of family-based immigration cases.

4. Modernizing the Visa System: The American Dream Act also sought to modernize the U.S. visa system by increasing the number of employment-based visas available each year

and eliminating per-country caps that had created long waiting times for applicants from certain countries. The bill also created a new visa category for essential workers in industries such as agriculture, healthcare, and technology.

5. Addressing the Root Causes of Migration: Recognizing that many migrants came to the United States to escape violence, poverty, and instability in their home countries, the bill included provisions to address the root causes of migration from Central America and other regions. This included increased funding for development assistance, anti-corruption initiatives, and security cooperation in countries like Guatemala, Honduras, and El Salvador.

6. Worker Protections: The bill included provisions to protect the rights of immigrant workers, including stronger enforcement of labor laws, protections against workplace discrimination, and access to legal representation for workers facing exploitation or abuse.

The American Dream Act was met with strong support from immigrant advocacy groups, civil rights organizations, and progressive lawmakers. Many saw the bill as a long-overdue step toward providing justice and opportunity for millions of undocumented immigrants who had been living in the shadows.

However, the bill also faced significant opposition, particularly from conservative lawmakers who argued that it amounted to "amnesty" for individuals who had violated U.S. immigration laws. Some critics also expressed concerns about the potential impact of the bill on the U.S. labor market, as well as the cost of implementing the reforms.

The administration launched an extensive campaign to build support for the American Dream Act, both within Congress and among the public. Harris personally met with key lawmakers, community leaders, and business representatives to discuss the importance of the bill and to address concerns. She emphasized that providing a pathway to citizenship was not only a matter of justice but also a practical solution to the challenges facing the U.S. immigration system.

The Legislative Battle

The legislative battle over the American Dream Act was intense and often contentious. While the bill had strong support from Democrats in both the House and the Senate, it faced stiff opposition from Republicans, particularly in the Senate where the filibuster remained a significant hurdle.

Harris and her administration worked tirelessly to build a bipartisan coalition in support of the bill. This included making concessions to moderate Republicans, such as increasing funding for border security and tightening eligibility requirements for the pathway to citizenship. However, these concessions also drew criticism from some progressives who argued that the bill did not go far enough in protecting the rights of immigrants.

The administration also faced challenges from within the Democratic Party, particularly from lawmakers representing districts with large immigrant populations who pushed for more expansive reforms. Harris had to navigate these internal divisions carefully, balancing the need for compromise with the desire to deliver meaningful change.

The turning point in the legislative battle came when a group of moderate Republicans, led by Senator Susan Collins of Maine, announced their support for the American Dream Act. This gave the administration the 60 votes needed to overcome the filibuster and move the bill forward in the Senate.

The American Dream Act passed the Senate by a narrow margin, with Vice President Tim Walz casting the tie-breaking vote in favor of the bill. The House of Representatives, where Democrats held a more substantial majority, passed the bill with a wider margin, although there were still defections from both sides of the aisle.

The passage of the American Dream Act was a significant victory for the Harris administration and a major step forward in the effort to reform the U.S. immigration system. The bill provided a pathway to citizenship for millions of undocumented immigrants, while also addressing key issues such as family reunification, worker protections, and the root causes of migration.

Addressing the Border Crisis: A New Approach to Security and Humanitarian Concerns

While the passage of the American Dream Act was a significant achievement, the Harris administration also faced the ongoing challenge of managing the U.S.-Mexico border. The border had become a focal point of national debate, with concerns about illegal immigration, drug trafficking, and national security often clashing with the humanitarian needs of migrants fleeing violence and poverty.

Harris's approach to border policy was guided by two key principles: ensuring national security and treating migrants with dignity and respect. She believed that the United States could achieve both goals through a combination of effective border management, investment in border infrastructure, and the implementation of humane policies that prioritized the protection of vulnerable individuals.

The Border Crisis: Causes and Consequences

The border crisis was driven by a complex set of factors, including economic instability, violence, and political corruption in Central America, as well as long-standing issues within the U.S. immigration system. Many of the migrants arriving at the U.S.-Mexico border were fleeing dangerous conditions in their home countries, and they often undertook perilous journeys in search of safety and opportunity.

The previous administration's approach to the border had been characterized by a focus on deterrence, including the construction of a border wall, the implementation of "zero tolerance" policies, and the separation of families. These policies had been widely criticized for their harshness and their failure to address the root causes of migration.

Harris's administration sought to take a different approach, one that emphasized both security and humanity. This approach included several key components:

1. Comprehensive Border Management: The administration implemented a comprehensive border management strategy that included increased funding for border security, the use of advanced technology to monitor and secure the border, and the hiring of additional border patrol agents. However, Harris made it clear that border security would not come at the expense of human rights.

2. Ending Family Separation: One of the administration's first actions was to end the practice of family separation at the border, which had been widely condemned as inhumane. The administration implemented new guidelines to ensure that families arriving at the border would be kept together and that children would not be detained in unsuitable conditions.

3. Reforming Asylum Processing: The administration also sought to reform the asylum processing system to make it more efficient and humane. This included increasing funding for immigration courts, hiring more judges and asylum officers, and expanding access to legal representation for asylum seekers. The goal was to reduce the backlog of asylum cases and to ensure that those with legitimate claims were granted protection.

4. Creating Safe and Legal Pathways: Recognizing that many migrants were fleeing dangerous conditions, the

administration worked to create safe and legal pathways for individuals to apply for asylum and other forms of protection. This included expanding the Central American Minors Program, which allowed children from Central America to apply for asylum from their home countries, as well as increasing refugee resettlement numbers.

Challenges and Criticism

Despite the administration's efforts to address the border crisis in a humane and effective way, the issue remained deeply divisive and politically charged. Harris faced criticism from both sides of the aisle, as well as from immigrant advocacy groups and the public.

On the right, critics argued that the administration's policies were too lenient and would encourage more illegal immigration. They pointed to the increase in migrant arrivals at the border as evidence that the administration's approach was not working. Some lawmakers called for a return to the more aggressive deterrence policies of the previous administration, including the construction of additional border walls and the expansion of detention facilities.

On the left, immigrant advocacy groups and progressive lawmakers expressed concerns that the administration was not doing enough to protect the rights of migrants and to end harmful practices such as detention and deportation. They called for a more radical overhaul of the immigration system, including the abolition of Immigration and Customs Enforcement (ICE) and the closure of detention centers.

Harris and her administration had to navigate these competing pressures carefully, working to find a balance between security and humanitarian concerns. The administration also faced practical challenges in implementing its policies, including the ongoing strain on the asylum processing system, the difficulties of coordinating with foreign governments, and the logistical challenges of managing a large and complex border.

Political and Social Ramifications

The administration's immigration and border policies had significant political and social ramifications within the United States. Immigration had long been a polarizing issue, and the Harris administration's efforts to reform the system and address the border crisis were no exception.

The Political Landscape

Politically, the administration's immigration policies became a key point of contention between Democrats and Republicans. While Democrats largely supported the administration's approach, Republicans were almost uniformly opposed, arguing that the policies were too lenient and that they would lead to increased illegal immigration.

The debate over immigration reform and border security played out in Congress, where the administration faced significant challenges in passing its legislative agenda. While the American Dream Act was a major victory for the administration, other immigration-related bills, including proposals to increase funding for border security and to expand legal immigration pathways, faced strong opposition and were stalled in the Senate.

The issue of immigration also became a central theme in the 2026 midterm elections, with Republicans using the border crisis as a key campaign issue. The GOP argued that the administration's policies had led to a "border crisis" and that they were putting American security at risk. Democrats, on the other hand, defended the administration's approach, arguing that it was a humane and pragmatic solution to a complex issue.

The midterm elections were closely contested, with immigration playing a significant role in several key races. While Democrats were able to maintain control of the House of Representatives, they lost several seats in the Senate, making it even more difficult for the administration to advance its legislative agenda.

The Social Impact

The administration's immigration policies also had a profound social impact, particularly in communities with large immigrant populations. The pathway to citizenship provided by the American Dream Act was a source of hope and relief for millions of undocumented immigrants, many of whom had lived in fear of deportation for years.

For DREAMers, the passage of the American Dream Act was particularly significant. Many had lived in the United States for most of their lives and considered themselves American in every way except for their legal status. The act provided them with the opportunity to finally achieve legal status and to fully participate in the society they called home.

The administration's efforts to reform the asylum system and to create safe and legal pathways for migrants also had a significant impact on vulnerable populations. The expansion of refugee resettlement programs and the creation of new avenues for asylum seekers provided protection to thousands of individuals fleeing violence and persecution.

However, the social impact of the administration's policies was not universally positive. The ongoing challenges at the border, including the backlog of asylum cases and the strain on resources, continued to create difficult conditions for many migrants. The use of detention facilities, even in a more limited capacity, remained a contentious issue, with advocacy groups calling for the end of detention altogether.

The administration's focus on addressing the root causes of migration also had a broader social impact, particularly in Central America. The increased funding for development assistance, anti-corruption initiatives, and security cooperation helped to stabilize some regions and to reduce the push factors driving migration. However, these efforts were long-term in nature, and the results were not immediately apparent.

MADAM PRESIDENT: THE FIRST TERM OF KAMALA HARRIS

The Legacy of the Harris Administration's Immigration and Border Policies

As Kamala Harris's presidency progressed, the administration's immigration and border policies continued to evolve in response to changing circumstances and ongoing challenges. While the administration achieved significant successes, including the passage of the American Dream Act and the reform of the asylum system, it also faced ongoing difficulties in managing the border crisis and navigating the political and social ramifications of its policies.

The legacy of the Harris administration's immigration and border policies was complex and multifaceted. On one hand, the administration made significant strides in providing a pathway to citizenship for millions of undocumented immigrants, reforming the asylum system, and addressing the root causes of migration. These achievements were seen as major steps forward in the effort to create a more just and humane immigration system.

On the other hand, the administration's efforts were also marked by ongoing challenges and criticisms. The border crisis remained a persistent issue, and the administration faced criticism from both the left and the right for its handling of the situation. The political polarization surrounding immigration made it difficult to achieve comprehensive reform, and many of the administration's more ambitious proposals were stalled in Congress.

Ultimately, the Harris administration's immigration and border policies reflected the complexities of governing in a deeply divided country and a rapidly changing world. Harris's commitment to a humane and pragmatic approach to immigration, coupled with her efforts to balance security concerns with the protection of vulnerable populations, left a lasting impact on the U.S. immigration system and the lives of millions of immigrants.

As the nation looked to the future, the challenges of immigration and border policy remained, but the foundations laid by the Harris administration provided a roadmap for future efforts to create a more just, secure, and inclusive immigration system.

Chapter 10: Education and Innovation

A Vision for the Future of American Education

Education has always been at the heart of the American Dream—the belief that everyone, regardless of their background, should have the opportunity to achieve their full potential. For Kamala Harris, the first woman, the first Black person, and the first person of South Asian descent to become President of the United States, education was not just a policy priority; it was a personal mission. Harris understood that the future of the nation depended on the ability to provide high-quality education to all its citizens, preparing them for the challenges and opportunities of the 21st century.

As President, Harris was determined to lead a transformation in American education, one that would address longstanding inequalities, expand access to higher education, and ensure that every child had the tools they needed to succeed. Her administration's education reform efforts were guided by a vision of inclusivity, innovation, and investment in the future. From universal pre-K to vocational training, from teacher support to the integration of technology in classrooms, Harris's education agenda sought to build a system that was not only more equitable but also more dynamic and responsive to the needs of a rapidly changing world.

Expanding Access to Higher Education: A New Pathway to Opportunity

One of the cornerstones of Harris's education reform agenda was expanding access to higher education. Harris believed that in an increasingly complex and competitive global economy, higher education was more important than ever for individuals seeking to improve their economic prospects and contribute to the nation's prosperity. However, she also recognized that the rising cost of college had placed higher education out of reach for many Americans, particularly those from low-income and marginalized communities.

The College for All Initiative

To address these challenges, Harris introduced the College for All Initiative, a comprehensive plan aimed at making higher education more affordable and accessible for all Americans. The initiative included several key components:

1. Tuition-Free Community College: One of the central elements of the College for All Initiative was the provision of tuition-free community college for all students. Harris believed that community colleges played a vital role in providing affordable, high-quality education and training opportunities, particularly for students who might not have the financial resources to attend a four-year university. Under the initiative, the federal government partnered with

states to cover the cost of tuition for students attending public community colleges.

2. Expanded Pell Grants: The initiative also included a significant expansion of the federal Pell Grant program, which provides need-based financial aid to low-income students. Harris's plan increased the maximum Pell Grant award and expanded eligibility to cover more students, including those from middle-income families who were struggling to afford college. The expanded Pell Grants could be used to cover not only tuition but also other expenses such as books, transportation, and housing.

3. Debt-Free College: Harris was acutely aware of the burden of student loan debt on millions of Americans, many of whom were struggling to pay off their loans while trying to build their careers and support their families. As part of the College for All Initiative, Harris introduced measures to make public colleges and universities debt-free for students from low- and middle-income families. This included a combination of increased financial aid, state and federal funding, and efforts to reduce the overall cost of college attendance.

4. Support for Minority-Serving Institutions: Recognizing the important role that Historically Black Colleges and Universities (HBCUs), Hispanic-Serving Institutions (HSIs), and other Minority-Serving Institutions (MSIs) played in educating students from underrepresented communities, Harris's plan included increased funding and support for these institutions. The initiative provided grants

for infrastructure improvements, faculty development, and student support services, helping to ensure that MSIs could continue to offer high-quality education to their students.

5. Strengthening Vocational and Technical Education: The College for All Initiative also emphasized the importance of vocational and technical education as a pathway to well-paying jobs and economic mobility. Harris's plan included increased funding for career and technical education (CTE) programs at community colleges, high schools, and vocational training centers. The initiative aimed to expand access to CTE programs in high-demand fields such as healthcare, technology, and advanced manufacturing.

The Impact of the College for All Initiative

The College for All Initiative was a transformative step in making higher education more accessible and affordable for millions of Americans. By providing tuition-free community college and expanding financial aid, the initiative helped to reduce the financial barriers that had prevented many students from pursuing higher education.

The expansion of Pell Grants and the introduction of debt-free college options provided significant relief to low- and middle-income students, many of whom had previously taken on substantial debt to pay for their education. The initiative also had a particularly positive impact on students from underrepresented communities, including those attending HBCUs, HSIs, and other MSIs.

Vocational and technical education programs saw a surge in enrollment as a result of the increased funding and support provided by the initiative. These programs provided students with the skills and credentials needed to succeed in high-demand industries, helping to address the nation's workforce needs and reduce unemployment.

While the College for All Initiative was widely praised for its ambitious goals and its potential to expand educational opportunities, it also faced challenges and criticisms. Some critics argued that the initiative was too costly and that it would place an undue burden on taxpayers. Others questioned whether the focus on community colleges and vocational education would adequately prepare students for the demands of the modern economy.

Despite these challenges, the College for All Initiative represented a significant step forward in the effort to make higher education more accessible and equitable. Harris's commitment to expanding educational opportunities for all Americans was a central element of her administration's broader vision for a more just and prosperous society.

Universal Pre-K: Laying the Foundation for Lifelong Learning

In addition to expanding access to higher education, Harris's administration placed a strong emphasis on early childhood education, recognizing that the first years of a child's life are critical to their long-term development and success. Harris believed that providing universal access to high-quality pre-K was one of the most effective ways to close the achievement gap, promote equity, and ensure that every child had the opportunity to reach their full potential.

The Universal Pre-K Initiative

Harris's Universal Pre-K Initiative aimed to provide free, high-quality pre-kindergarten education to all 3- and 4-year-olds in the United States. The initiative was based on the belief that early childhood education was not just a privilege but a right, and that investing in young children was one of the most effective ways to build a strong foundation for lifelong learning.

The Universal Pre-K Initiative included several key components:

1. **Federal and State Partnership:** The initiative was designed as a federal-state partnership, with the federal government providing funding and support to states to expand access to pre-K programs. States were required to develop and implement their own pre-K programs, with the federal government providing matching funds to cover the cost of tuition and other expenses.

2. High-Quality Standards: The initiative emphasized the importance of high-quality early childhood education, with a focus on small class sizes, well-trained teachers, and evidence-based curricula. The federal government provided guidelines and support to help states develop and implement high-quality pre-K programs, with an emphasis on ensuring

that all children had access to a nurturing and stimulating learning environment.

3. Inclusive and Culturally Responsive Education: The initiative prioritized inclusivity and cultural responsiveness, recognizing the diverse backgrounds and experiences of young children in the United States. The federal government provided funding and support for programs that served children from low-income families, children with disabilities, and children who were English language learners. The initiative also encouraged the development of curricula and teaching practices that reflected the cultural and linguistic diversity of the students.

4. Support for Teachers: The initiative recognized the critical role that early childhood educators played in the success of pre-K programs. To support teachers, the initiative included increased funding for teacher training and professional development, as well as efforts to improve compensation and working conditions for pre-K teachers. The goal was to attract and retain high-quality educators who were committed to providing the best possible education for young children.

5. Family Engagement: The initiative emphasized the importance of family engagement in early childhood education, recognizing that parents and caregivers were essential partners in their children's learning. The federal government provided funding and support for programs that encouraged family involvement, including parent

education, home visits, and opportunities for parents to participate in their children's education.

The Impact of Universal Pre-K

The Universal Pre-K Initiative had a profound impact on early childhood education in the United States. By providing free, high-quality pre-K to all 3- and 4-year-olds, the initiative helped to close the achievement gap and ensure that all children, regardless of their background, had the opportunity to start school ready to learn.

The initiative was particularly beneficial for children from low-income families, who often lacked access to high-quality early childhood education. Research had shown that children who attended high-quality pre-K programs were more likely to succeed in school, graduate from high school, and go on to college or a career. The Universal Pre-K Initiative helped to level the playing field for these children, providing them with the foundation they needed to succeed.

The initiative also had a positive impact on families, particularly working parents who often struggled to find affordable and reliable childcare. By providing free pre-K, the initiative reduced the financial burden on families and allowed parents to pursue their own education and career goals.

While the Universal Pre-K Initiative was widely praised for its ambitious goals and its potential to improve educational outcomes, it also faced challenges in implementation. Some states struggled to expand their pre-K programs to meet the demand, while others faced challenges in maintaining high-quality standards. The federal government worked closely with states to address these challenges, providing technical assistance and support to ensure that the initiative was successful.

Improving Public School Funding: Investing in the Future

Another key component of Harris's education reform agenda was improving public school funding. Harris believed that every child, regardless of where they lived, should have access to a high-quality public education. However, she also recognized that the existing funding system was deeply inequitable, with significant disparities in funding levels between wealthy and low-income districts.

The Fair Funding for Public Schools Act

To address these disparities, Harris introduced the Fair Funding for Public Schools Act, a comprehensive plan aimed at ensuring that all public schools received the resources they needed to provide a high-quality education to their students. The act included several key components:

1. Increased Federal Funding: The act provided a significant increase in federal funding for public schools, with a focus on supporting schools in low-income and underfunded districts. The federal government provided additional funding for Title I schools, which served a high percentage of low-income students, as well as for schools in rural and underserved communities.

2. Equitable Funding Formulas: The act required states to develop and implement more equitable funding formulas that ensured that resources were distributed based on student need. This included taking into account factors such as poverty levels, English language proficiency, and special education needs. States that failed to adopt equitable funding formulas risked losing federal funding.

3. Modernizing School Facilities: The act included funding for the modernization and repair of school facilities, many of which were outdated and in poor condition. The federal government provided grants to states and districts to upgrade school buildings, improve technology infrastructure, and create safe and healthy learning environments.

4. Supporting Teachers and Staff: The act included increased funding for teacher salaries, professional development, and classroom resources. The goal was to attract and retain high-quality educators and to provide them with the support they needed to succeed. The act also included funding for hiring additional support staff, such as counselors, nurses, and social workers, to address the social and emotional needs of students.

5. Addressing Racial and Economic Disparities: The act emphasized the importance of addressing racial and economic disparities in education. It included funding for programs that aimed to close the achievement gap, reduce dropout rates, and increase college readiness among students of color and low-income students. The act also required

states and districts to report on their progress in addressing these disparities.

The Impact of the Fair Funding for Public Schools Act

The Fair Funding for Public Schools Act was a significant step forward in the effort to create a more equitable and effective public education system. By increasing federal funding and promoting more equitable funding formulas, the act helped to ensure that all students, regardless of their background, had access to the resources they needed to succeed.

The act had a particularly positive impact on low-income and underfunded districts, many of which had struggled for years to provide a high-quality education with limited resources. The increased funding allowed these districts to hire more teachers, reduce class sizes, and invest in technology and infrastructure. As a result, students in these districts saw improvements in academic achievement, graduation rates, and college readiness.

The act also helped to address longstanding disparities in education by providing targeted support for students of color and low-income students. Programs aimed at closing the achievement gap and increasing college readiness helped to level the playing field for these students, providing them with the opportunities they needed to succeed.

While the Fair Funding for Public Schools Act was widely praised for its potential to improve public education, it also faced challenges in implementation. Some states and districts struggled to meet the requirements of the act, particularly in developing and implementing equitable funding formulas. The federal government worked closely with states to address these challenges, providing technical assistance and support to ensure that the act was successful.

Supporting Teachers: The Heart of Education Reform

Harris recognized that teachers were the heart of the education system, and that any effort to improve education would need to focus on supporting and empowering educators. Throughout her presidency, Harris made it a priority to address the challenges facing teachers, including low pay, limited resources, and a lack of professional development opportunities.

The Teacher Support and Empowerment Act

To support teachers, Harris introduced the Teacher Support and Empowerment Act, a comprehensive plan aimed at improving teacher compensation, providing professional development opportunities, and creating a more supportive working environment for educators.

The Teacher Support and Empowerment Act included several key components:

1. Increased Teacher Pay: The act provided federal funding to increase teacher salaries, with a focus on raising pay for teachers in low-income and underfunded districts. The goal was to attract and retain high-quality educators and to

ensure that teaching was a financially viable career option for individuals from diverse backgrounds.

2. Professional Development: The act included funding for professional development programs that provided teachers with the training and support they needed to succeed in the classroom. This included opportunities for teachers to pursue advanced degrees, participate in mentoring and coaching programs, and attend workshops and conferences. The act also emphasized the importance of ongoing professional development to help teachers stay current with best practices and new developments in education.

3. Classroom Resources: The act provided funding for classroom resources, including textbooks, technology, and instructional materials. The goal was to ensure that teachers had the tools they needed to provide a high-quality education to their students. The act also included funding for the development of culturally responsive curricula that reflected the diverse backgrounds and experiences of students.

4. Addressing Teacher Shortages: The act included measures to address teacher shortages in critical subject areas, such as math, science, and special education. This included funding for teacher recruitment and retention programs, as well as scholarships and loan forgiveness programs for individuals pursuing careers in teaching.

5. Creating Supportive Working Environments: The act emphasized the importance of creating supportive working

environments for teachers. This included funding for programs that promoted teacher collaboration, reduced administrative burdens, and provided support for teachers' mental health and well-being. The act also encouraged schools and districts to implement policies that promoted work-life balance and prevented teacher burnout.

The Impact of the Teacher Support and Empowerment Act

The Teacher Support and Empowerment Act had a significant impact on the teaching profession in the United States. By increasing teacher pay and providing funding for professional development, the act helped to attract and retain high-quality educators and to ensure that teachers had the support they needed to succeed in the classroom.

The act was particularly beneficial for teachers in low-income and underfunded districts, many of whom had struggled with low pay, limited resources, and challenging working conditions. The increased funding allowed these districts to offer competitive salaries, reduce class sizes, and provide teachers with the tools and support they needed to provide a high-quality education to their students.

The act also helped to address teacher shortages in critical subject areas, such as math, science, and special education. The funding for teacher recruitment and retention programs, as well as scholarships and loan forgiveness programs, encouraged more individuals to pursue careers in teaching and helped to fill gaps in the teaching workforce.

While the Teacher Support and Empowerment Act was widely praised for its potential to improve the teaching profession, it also faced challenges in implementation. Some districts struggled to meet the requirements of the act, particularly in providing professional development opportunities and creating supportive working environments for teachers. The federal government worked closely with states and districts to address these challenges, providing technical assistance and support to ensure that the act was successful.

The Role of Technology in Education: Shaping the Future of Learning

As President, Harris was keenly aware of the transformative potential of technology in education. She believed that technology could play a critical role in expanding access to education, personalizing learning, and preparing students for the demands of the modern economy. However, she also recognized that the integration of technology in education needed to be done thoughtfully and equitably, with a focus on ensuring that all students had access to the tools and resources they needed to succeed.

The Future of Learning Initiative

To harness the potential of technology in education, Harris introduced the Future of Learning Initiative, a comprehensive plan aimed at integrating technology into the classroom in a way that enhanced learning and promoted equity. The initiative included several key components:

1. Expanding Access to Technology: The initiative provided funding to expand access to technology in schools, particularly in low-income and underfunded districts. This included funding for devices such as laptops and tablets, as well as for high-speed internet access and technology infrastructure. The goal was to ensure that all students had access to the tools they needed to participate in digital learning.

2. Personalized Learning: The initiative emphasized the importance of personalized learning, using technology to tailor instruction to the individual needs and interests of students. This included funding for the development of adaptive learning platforms and digital curricula that allowed students to learn at their own pace and to pursue subjects that interested them.

3. Teacher Training in Technology: The initiative included funding for teacher training in the use of technology in the classroom. This included opportunities for teachers to learn how to integrate technology into their instruction, use digital tools to assess student progress, and create engaging and interactive learning experiences. The goal was to ensure that teachers were equipped with the skills and knowledge they needed to effectively use technology in their teaching.

4. Promoting Digital Literacy: The initiative emphasized the importance of digital literacy, recognizing that students needed to be able to navigate and critically evaluate digital information in order to succeed in the modern economy. The initiative provided funding for programs that taught

students digital literacy skills, including how to use technology safely and responsibly, how to evaluate the credibility of online sources, and how to protect their privacy and security online.

5. Addressing the Digital Divide: The initiative recognized that the digital divide—the gap between those who had access to technology and those who did not—was a significant barrier to educational equity. The initiative included funding for programs that aimed to close the digital divide, including efforts to expand internet access in rural and underserved communities and to provide devices and technology support to low-income families.

The Impact of the Future of Learning Initiative

The Future of Learning Initiative had a transformative impact on education in the United States. By expanding access to technology and promoting personalized learning, the initiative helped to create more engaging and effective learning experiences for students.

The initiative was particularly beneficial for students in low-income and underfunded districts, many of whom had previously lacked access to the technology and resources needed to succeed in the digital age. The increased funding for devices, internet access, and technology infrastructure helped to level the playing field for these students, providing them with the tools they needed to participate fully in digital learning.

The initiative also helped to prepare students for the demands of the modern economy by promoting digital literacy and teaching students the skills they needed to navigate the digital world. The focus on personalized learning allowed students to take ownership of their education, pursue their interests, and develop the skills and knowledge they needed to succeed in the future.

While the Future of Learning Initiative was widely praised for its potential to transform education, it also faced challenges in implementation. Some schools and districts struggled to integrate technology into their instruction, particularly in areas where teachers lacked the necessary training and support. The federal government worked closely with states and districts to address these challenges, providing technical assistance and support to ensure that the initiative was successful.

A Legacy of Education and Innovation

As Kamala Harris's presidency progressed, her administration's education reform efforts left a lasting impact on the U.S. education system. From expanding access to higher education to promoting universal pre-K, from improving public school funding to supporting teachers, and from harnessing the power of technology to addressing the digital divide, Harris's education agenda was comprehensive and ambitious.

The initiatives introduced by Harris and her administration helped to create a more equitable and effective education system, providing students with the opportunities and resources they needed to succeed in the 21st century. The focus on inclusivity, innovation, and investment in the future reflected Harris's belief that education was the key to unlocking the potential of every individual and to building a more just and prosperous society.

While the administration's education reform efforts faced challenges and criticisms, the progress made under Harris's leadership was undeniable. The expansion of access to higher education, the implementation of universal pre-K, the improvement of public school funding, the support for teachers, and the integration of technology in education all contributed to a more dynamic and responsive education system.

As the nation looked to the future, the legacy of Harris's education and innovation initiatives provided a roadmap for continued progress in the effort to ensure that every American had the opportunity to achieve their full potential through education. The reforms introduced during Harris's presidency laid the foundation for a more inclusive, equitable, and innovative education system, one that would prepare future generations to thrive in a rapidly changing world.

Chapter 11: Women's Rights and Gender Equality

A New Era for Women's Rights

Kamala Harris's presidency marked a historic turning point for women's rights and gender equality in the United States and around the world. As the first woman, the first Black woman, and the first person of South Asian descent to hold the office of President, Harris's rise to the highest political position in the United States was more than symbolic—it was a powerful affirmation of the possibilities for women everywhere. Her leadership offered a profound statement about the breaking of barriers and the progress toward true gender equality.

From the moment she took office, Harris made it clear that advancing women's rights and gender equality would be central to her administration's agenda. Harris understood that despite the significant progress made in recent decades, women continued to face systemic barriers to equality in nearly every aspect of life—from the workplace to healthcare, from the justice system to the political arena. She also recognized that the challenges facing women were intersectional, meaning that race, class, sexuality, and other identities played critical roles in shaping women's experiences of inequality.

Harris's approach to gender equality was comprehensive and far-reaching, encompassing a wide range of initiatives aimed at addressing the most pressing issues facing women in the United States and around the world. These efforts included combating gender-based violence, ensuring pay equity, defending reproductive rights, and advancing women's leadership. Under Harris's leadership, the administration sought not only to rectify the injustices that women faced but also to create a society in which women could thrive as equals, fully empowered to pursue their goals and dreams.

Pay Equity: Closing the Wage Gap

One of the central pillars of Harris's agenda for women's rights was the fight for pay equity. Despite decades of progress, women in the United States continued to earn less than men for doing the same work. The gender pay gap was even more pronounced for women of color, with Black women, Latinas, and Native American women facing some of the widest wage disparities. Harris believed that achieving pay equity was not only a matter of fairness but also essential for the economic security and well-being of women and their families.

The Pay Equity Act

To address the persistent gender pay gap, Harris introduced the Pay Equity Act, a comprehensive bill aimed at ensuring equal pay for equal work. The Pay Equity Act included several key provisions designed to close the wage gap and promote transparency in the workplace:

1. Prohibiting Pay Discrimination: The Pay Equity Act strengthened existing laws prohibiting pay discrimination based on gender. It closed loopholes in the Equal Pay Act of 1963, which had allowed employers to justify pay disparities based on factors unrelated to job performance. The new law required that any differences in pay between men and women performing the same work must be based on legitimate business reasons, such as education, experience, or performance, rather than on gender.

2. Pay Transparency: One of the most significant provisions of the Pay Equity Act was the requirement for pay transparency. Under the law, employers were required to disclose salary ranges for job openings and provide employees with information about their own pay relative to their colleagues. This provision was designed to prevent wage discrimination and give employees the information they needed to advocate for fair pay.

3. Banning Salary History Inquiries: The Pay Equity Act also banned employers from asking job applicants about their salary history. Harris recognized that the practice of using salary history to set pay often perpetuated existing wage disparities, particularly for women and people of color. By prohibiting salary history inquiries, the law aimed to ensure that employees were paid based on their qualifications and the value of their work, rather than on their past earnings.

4. Strengthening Enforcement: The Pay Equity Act provided additional resources for the enforcement of pay discrimination laws. This included increased funding for the

Equal Employment Opportunity Commission (EEOC) to investigate pay discrimination claims and expanded protections for employees who filed complaints. The law also established penalties for employers who violated pay equity requirements, including fines and back pay for affected employees.

5. Supporting Pay Equity Audits: The Pay Equity Act encouraged employers to conduct pay equity audits to identify and address wage disparities within their organizations. The law provided incentives for companies to voluntarily review their pay practices and make adjustments to ensure that employees were paid fairly. Employers who conducted pay equity audits and took corrective action were eligible for tax credits and other benefits.

The Impact of the Pay Equity Act

The Pay Equity Act was a landmark piece of legislation in the fight for gender equality in the workplace. By strengthening protections against pay discrimination, promoting transparency, and eliminating practices that perpetuated wage disparities, the law helped to close the gender pay gap and ensure that women were paid fairly for their work.

The requirement for pay transparency had a particularly significant impact on reducing wage disparities. With access to information about salary ranges and their colleagues' pay, employees were better equipped to negotiate fair compensation and hold their employers accountable for any discrepancies. The ban on salary history inquiries also helped to break the cycle of wage inequality by ensuring that pay was based on qualifications and job performance, rather than on past earnings.

The Pay Equity Act was also instrumental in addressing wage disparities for women of color, who had long faced some of the widest pay gaps. By targeting the root causes of pay discrimination and providing tools for enforcement and accountability, the law helped to create a more level playing field for all women, regardless of their race or ethnicity.

Despite the significant progress made under the Pay Equity Act, challenges remained. Some employers resisted the requirements for pay transparency, citing concerns about privacy and competitiveness. Additionally, the enforcement of pay equity laws continued to face obstacles, including limited resources for investigating complaints and the difficulty of proving pay discrimination in some cases. However, the Pay Equity Act represented a major step forward in the ongoing struggle for economic justice and gender equality in the workplace.

Reproductive Rights: Defending Women's Autonomy

Reproductive rights were another central focus of Harris's agenda for women's rights. As a longtime advocate for reproductive freedom, Harris was committed to ensuring that all women had the ability to make decisions about their own bodies and access the healthcare services they needed. She recognized that reproductive rights were not only a matter of personal autonomy but also essential for women's health, economic security, and equality.

The Women's Health Protection Act

One of the key pieces of legislation championed by Harris was the Women's Health Protection Act, a bill designed to protect and expand access to reproductive healthcare, including abortion services. The Women's Health Protection Act included several key provisions:

1. Protecting Access to Abortion: The Women's Health Protection Act sought to protect the right to access abortion services by preventing states from enacting restrictive laws that imposed unnecessary barriers to care. The law prohibited states from implementing measures such as mandatory waiting periods, medically unnecessary ultrasounds, and excessive regulations on abortion providers. The goal was to ensure that women could access safe and legal abortion services without undue burden or delay.

2. Codifying Roe v. Wade: The Women's Health Protection Act codified the protections established by the Supreme Court's decision in Roe v. Wade, which recognized the constitutional right to abortion. By enshrining these protections in federal law, the act aimed to safeguard reproductive rights against future legal challenges and ensure that all women, regardless of where they lived, had access to abortion services.

3. Expanding Access to Reproductive Healthcare: In addition to protecting abortion rights, the Women's Health Protection Act also included provisions to expand access to a range of reproductive healthcare services. This included funding for family planning programs, comprehensive sex education, and preventive care such as contraception and cancer screenings. The law aimed to ensure that all women had access to the full spectrum of reproductive healthcare services, regardless of their income or geographic location.

4. Addressing Health Disparities: The Women's Health Protection Act recognized the significant disparities in reproductive healthcare access and outcomes experienced by women of color, low-income women, and women in rural areas. The law included funding for community health centers and other healthcare providers that served underserved populations, as well as initiatives to address the social determinants of health that contributed to these disparities.

5. Protecting Healthcare Providers: The Women's Health Protection Act included protections for healthcare providers who offered abortion services and other reproductive healthcare. The law aimed to prevent harassment, intimidation, and violence against providers and to ensure that they could practice without fear of legal or physical threats.

The Impact of the Women's Health Protection Act

The Women's Health Protection Act was a critical victory for reproductive rights advocates and a major step forward in the fight to protect and expand access to reproductive healthcare. By codifying the protections established by Roe v. Wade and preventing states from enacting restrictive laws, the act helped to ensure that all women had the ability to make decisions about their own bodies and access the care they needed.

The act also played a significant role in addressing health disparities and expanding access to reproductive healthcare for underserved populations. By providing funding for community health centers and other healthcare providers, the law helped to ensure that women in rural areas, low-income women, and women of color had access to the full range of reproductive healthcare services.

Despite the success of the Women's Health Protection Act, Harris's administration faced significant opposition from anti-abortion activists and conservative lawmakers. Efforts to challenge the law in the courts and at the state level continued, highlighting the ongoing struggle to protect reproductive rights in the face of persistent opposition.

Combating Gender-Based Violence: A National Priority

Another key focus of Harris's agenda for women's rights was combating gender-based violence. Harris had long been an advocate for survivors of domestic violence, sexual assault, and other forms of gender-based violence, and she was committed to making this issue a national priority. She believed that no one should live in fear of violence and that the government had a responsibility to protect and support survivors.

The Violence Against Women Reauthorization Act

One of the cornerstone pieces of legislation championed by Harris was the reauthorization of the Violence Against Women Act (VAWA). Originally passed in 1994, VAWA had been a critical tool in addressing gender-based violence, providing funding for services and support for survivors, as well as resources for law enforcement and prevention efforts. However, VAWA had faced challenges in recent years, including lapses in authorization and efforts to weaken its protections.

Harris's administration worked to reauthorize and strengthen VAWA, ensuring that it remained a powerful tool in the fight against gender-based violence. The Violence Against Women Reauthorization Act included several key provisions:

1. Expanding Protections for Survivors: The reauthorization of VAWA expanded protections for survivors of gender-based violence, including extending protections to survivors of intimate partner violence, stalking, and sexual assault. The law also included provisions to protect survivors from being evicted or discriminated against by landlords based on their status as victims of violence.

2. Strengthening Services for Survivors: The Violence Against Women Reauthorization Act provided increased

funding for services and support for survivors, including shelters, counseling, legal assistance, and medical care. The law also expanded funding for culturally specific services and programs that addressed the unique needs of survivors from marginalized communities, including Native American women, LGBTQ+ individuals, and immigrants.

3. Enhancing Law Enforcement and Prosecution Efforts: The reauthorization of VAWA included funding and resources for law enforcement and prosecutors to better respond to cases of gender-based violence. This included training for police officers and prosecutors on handling domestic violence and sexual assault cases, as well as efforts to improve the coordination between law enforcement agencies and service providers.

4. Preventing Gender-Based Violence: The Violence Against Women Reauthorization Act included a renewed focus on prevention efforts, including funding for education and outreach programs that aimed to raise awareness about gender-based violence and promote healthy relationships. The law also supported initiatives to engage men and boys in efforts to prevent violence and promote gender equality.

5. Addressing Violence Against Native American Women: The reauthorization of VAWA included specific provisions to address the high rates of violence experienced by Native American women, including expanding the jurisdiction of tribal courts to prosecute non-Native offenders who committed acts of violence against Native women on tribal lands. The law also provided funding for tribal law

enforcement and service providers to better address the needs of Native survivors.

The Impact of the Violence Against Women Reauthorization Act

The reauthorization of the Violence Against Women Act was a critical achievement for Harris's administration and a significant step forward in the fight against gender-based violence. By expanding protections for survivors, strengthening services and support, and enhancing law enforcement and prevention efforts, the law helped to ensure that survivors received the care and justice they deserved.

The reauthorization of VAWA also played a crucial role in addressing the unique needs of survivors from marginalized communities, including Native American women, LGBTQ+ individuals, and immigrants. The law's focus on culturally specific services and programs helped to ensure that all survivors had access to the support they needed, regardless of their background or identity.

Despite the success of the Violence Against Women Reauthorization Act, the fight against gender-based violence remained an ongoing challenge. Harris's administration continued to work with advocates, service providers, and law enforcement to build on the progress made under VAWA and to address the root causes of gender-based violence.

Kamala Harris as a Role Model for Women in Leadership

MADAM PRESIDENT: THE FIRST TERM OF KAMALA HARRIS

Throughout her presidency, Kamala Harris served as a powerful role model for women in leadership, both in the United States and around the world. As the first woman to hold the office of President, Harris's leadership shattered the highest glass ceiling in American politics and sent a powerful message about the possibilities for women in leadership.

Inspiring a New Generation of Women Leaders

Harris's rise to the presidency inspired a new generation of women to pursue leadership roles in politics, business, and other fields. Her story resonated with women from all walks of life, particularly women of color, who saw in Harris a reflection of their own experiences and aspirations.

Harris's presidency also had a profound impact on the representation of women in politics. Her leadership encouraged more women to run for office at all levels of government, resulting in historic gains in women's representation in Congress, state legislatures, and local governments. The success of these women candidates helped to create a more diverse and representative government, one that better reflected the experiences and perspectives of all Americans.

In addition to inspiring women in the United States, Harris's leadership had a global impact. As one of the most powerful leaders in the world, Harris used her platform to advocate for women's rights and gender equality on the international stage. Her presidency provided a powerful example of what was possible for women in leadership and helped to elevate the status of women's rights as a global priority.

Championing Women's Leadership

Throughout her presidency, Harris made it a priority to champion women's leadership and to create opportunities for women to advance in their careers. This included appointing women to key positions in her administration, including the Cabinet, federal judiciary, and other high-level roles. Harris's commitment to gender parity in leadership positions helped to ensure that women's voices were represented at the highest levels of government.

Harris also worked to promote women's leadership in the private sector, including in business, technology, and finance. Her administration introduced initiatives to support women entrepreneurs, provide funding for women-led startups, and promote gender diversity in corporate leadership. These efforts helped to create more opportunities for women to succeed in traditionally male-dominated fields and to close the gender gap in leadership positions.

The Global Impact of Harris's Leadership

Harris's presidency had a significant impact on women's movements globally, particularly in countries where women continued to face significant barriers to equality and leadership. Harris used her platform to advocate for women's rights on the international stage, including at the United Nations, G7, and other global forums. Her leadership helped to elevate the status of women's rights as a global priority and to mobilize international support for gender equality initiatives.

In addition to her advocacy efforts, Harris also provided tangible support for women's rights organizations and movements around the world. Her administration increased funding for global women's rights initiatives, including programs that promoted women's political participation, economic empowerment, and access to education and healthcare. These efforts helped to advance gender equality in countries where women's rights had been historically marginalized.

Key Legislative Successes and Challenges

Harris's administration achieved several key legislative successes in advancing women's rights and gender equality, including the passage of the Pay Equity Act, the Women's Health Protection Act, and the Violence Against Women Reauthorization Act. These laws represented significant steps forward in the fight for gender equality and helped to address some of the most pressing issues facing women in the United States.

However, the administration also faced significant challenges in advancing its gender equality agenda. Efforts to pass additional legislation, such as the Equal Rights Amendment (ERA) and the Family and Medical Leave Act expansion, faced strong opposition in Congress and were ultimately unsuccessful. The administration also faced challenges in addressing the ongoing attacks on reproductive rights, particularly at the state level, where conservative lawmakers continued to pass restrictive laws aimed at limiting access to abortion and other reproductive healthcare services.

Despite these challenges, Harris's administration remained committed to advancing gender equality and women's rights. The progress made under her leadership provided a strong foundation for future efforts to create a more just and equal society for all women.

A Legacy of Equality and Empowerment

As Kamala Harris's presidency progressed, her administration's efforts to advance women's rights and gender equality left a lasting impact on the United States and the world. From fighting for pay equity to defending reproductive rights, from combating gender-based violence to championing women's leadership, Harris's commitment to gender equality was unwavering.

Harris's leadership not only advanced the cause of women's rights but also inspired a new generation of women leaders and activists. Her presidency shattered barriers and demonstrated that women could lead at the highest levels of government and beyond. Her impact on women's movements globally helped to elevate the status of gender equality as a priority on the international stage.

While challenges remained in the fight for gender equality, the progress made under Harris's leadership provided a roadmap for continued efforts to create a society where all women could thrive as equals. The legacy of Harris's presidency would be remembered as a time when the pursuit of gender equality took center stage and when the United States made significant strides toward a more just and equal future for all.

Chapter 12: Technology and Cybersecurity

Navigating the Digital Frontier: The Challenges of a Rapidly Evolving Landscape

As the 21st century progressed, technology increasingly defined nearly every aspect of modern life. The rise of the internet, the proliferation of smart devices, and the expansion of global digital networks had transformed how people communicated, conducted business, and even governed themselves. However, these advancements came with significant challenges, including cybersecurity threats, the spread of misinformation, and the growing power of tech monopolies. For President Kamala Harris, addressing these issues was crucial to ensuring that the digital age was one of progress and innovation rather than division and vulnerability.

Upon taking office, Harris was acutely aware of the rapidly evolving digital landscape and the complex issues it presented. She knew that to effectively govern in this new era, her administration would need to confront the challenges head-on while promoting technological innovation and safeguarding the rights and freedoms of citizens.

Cybersecurity: Protecting National Security and Public Trust

MADAM PRESIDENT: THE FIRST TERM OF KAMALA HARRIS

One of the most pressing concerns for the Harris administration was the issue of cybersecurity. As digital technologies became increasingly integrated into the fabric of society, the potential for cyberattacks to disrupt critical infrastructure, steal sensitive information, and undermine public trust grew exponentially. High-profile cyberattacks on government agencies, corporations, and even electoral systems had demonstrated the vulnerability of the nation's digital infrastructure and the need for a comprehensive cybersecurity strategy.

The National Cybersecurity Initiative

To address these threats, Harris launched the National Cybersecurity Initiative, a multi-faceted plan designed to protect the United States from cyberattacks, enhance the security of digital infrastructure, and build resilience against future threats. The initiative included several key components:

1. Strengthening Critical Infrastructure: The National Cybersecurity Initiative placed a strong emphasis on protecting critical infrastructure, such as the power grid, water supply systems, transportation networks, and financial institutions, from cyberattacks. The administration worked with public and private sector partners to conduct comprehensive risk assessments and implement advanced security measures to safeguard these vital systems. This included investing in encryption technologies, intrusion detection systems, and incident response protocols to prevent and mitigate the impact of cyberattacks.

2. Federal Cybersecurity Standards: Recognizing the need for consistent and robust cybersecurity practices across federal agencies, the Harris administration introduced new federal cybersecurity standards. These standards required agencies to adopt best practices in cybersecurity, including regular vulnerability assessments, multi-factor authentication, and continuous monitoring of networks. The administration also established a centralized cybersecurity oversight body, the Office of National Cybersecurity, to coordinate efforts across government agencies and ensure compliance with the new standards.

3. Cyber Threat Intelligence Sharing: To improve the nation's ability to detect and respond to cyber threats, the administration promoted greater collaboration between the government and the private sector in sharing cyber threat intelligence. The Cyber Threat Intelligence Sharing Act (CTISA) facilitated the real-time exchange of information about emerging threats, vulnerabilities, and attack vectors between government agencies, private companies, and international partners. This collaborative approach helped to identify and neutralize threats before they could cause significant harm.

4. Public-Private Partnerships: The Harris administration recognized that the private sector played a critical role in the nation's cybersecurity efforts, given that much of the country's digital infrastructure was owned and operated by private companies. To strengthen cybersecurity across all sectors, the administration fostered public-private partnerships that brought together government agencies,

tech companies, and industry leaders to develop and implement cybersecurity best practices. These partnerships also provided a forum for sharing information and resources to respond to cyber incidents quickly and effectively.

5. Cybersecurity Workforce Development: One of the challenges facing the nation's cybersecurity efforts was the shortage of skilled professionals in the field. To address this gap, the Harris administration launched a cybersecurity workforce development program that provided funding for education and training in cybersecurity. The program aimed to build a pipeline of cybersecurity professionals by supporting initiatives such as scholarships, apprenticeships, and certification programs. The administration also worked to increase diversity in the cybersecurity workforce, recognizing that a diverse and inclusive workforce would be better equipped to address the complex challenges of cybersecurity.

6. International Cybersecurity Cooperation: Cyber threats were not confined by national borders, and the Harris administration recognized the importance of international cooperation in addressing these challenges. The administration strengthened alliances with key international partners, including NATO and the European Union, to enhance collective cybersecurity efforts. This included joint exercises, information sharing, and the development of international norms and agreements to govern state behavior in cyberspace.

The Impact of the National Cybersecurity Initiative

The National Cybersecurity Initiative had a significant impact on the nation's ability to defend against cyber threats and protect critical infrastructure. By strengthening cybersecurity standards, enhancing threat intelligence sharing, and fostering public-private partnerships, the initiative helped to create a more resilient digital infrastructure capable of withstanding sophisticated cyberattacks.

One of the most notable successes of the initiative was its role in preventing a major cyberattack on the nation's power grid. In 2025, cybersecurity experts detected a sophisticated malware campaign targeting the control systems of multiple power plants across the country. Thanks to the advanced threat detection capabilities and coordinated response efforts established under the National Cybersecurity Initiative, the attack was thwarted before it could cause widespread damage.

The initiative also played a critical role in improving the cybersecurity practices of federal agencies. The adoption of new federal cybersecurity standards, coupled with increased oversight and accountability, led to a significant reduction in the number of successful cyberattacks on government networks. This, in turn, helped to restore public trust in the government's ability to protect sensitive information and maintain the integrity of its digital systems.

However, the initiative was not without its challenges. The rapidly evolving nature of cyber threats meant that the administration had to continuously adapt and update its strategies to stay ahead of malicious actors. Additionally, the reliance on public-private partnerships required careful coordination and collaboration, as private companies and government agencies often had different priorities and approaches to cybersecurity.

Despite these challenges, the National Cybersecurity Initiative was widely regarded as a critical achievement of the Harris administration and a key component of the nation's efforts to secure its digital future.

Regulating the Tech Industry: Addressing Monopolies and Misinformation

In addition to cybersecurity, another major focus of the Harris administration was the regulation of the tech industry. As technology companies grew in size and influence, concerns about their market power, control over personal data, and role in the spread of misinformation became increasingly prominent. Harris recognized that the unchecked power of tech monopolies posed a threat not only to competition but also to democracy itself. Her administration sought to address these issues through a combination of regulation, antitrust enforcement, and efforts to promote innovation and competition.

The Tech Accountability Act

One of the central pieces of legislation introduced by Harris to address the challenges posed by the tech industry was the Tech Accountability Act. This comprehensive bill aimed to regulate the behavior of tech companies, promote competition, and protect consumers and democracy from the negative impacts of tech monopolies and misinformation.

The Tech Accountability Act included several key provisions:

1. Antitrust Enforcement: The Tech Accountability Act strengthened antitrust laws to prevent tech companies from engaging in anti-competitive practices and abusing their market power. The law provided the Federal Trade Commission (FTC) and the Department of Justice (DOJ) with additional resources and authority to investigate and prosecute antitrust violations. It also introduced new rules to prevent tech companies from using mergers and acquisitions to stifle competition and consolidate their dominance in the market.

2. Data Privacy Protections: The Tech Accountability Act introduced robust data privacy protections to give consumers greater control over their personal information. The law required tech companies to obtain explicit consent from users before collecting, using, or sharing their data. It also mandated that companies provide clear and transparent information about their data practices and give users the ability to access, correct, and delete their data. The law established penalties for companies that violated these privacy protections, including fines and restrictions on data collection.

3. Transparency in Algorithms: One of the key concerns about tech companies was their use of algorithms to shape user experiences and influence behavior. The Tech Accountability Act introduced new transparency requirements for algorithms used by tech companies, particularly those that determined the content users saw on social media platforms, search engines, and other digital services. The law required companies to disclose how their algorithms worked, including the factors that influenced algorithmic decisions and the potential biases they introduced. This transparency aimed to hold companies accountable for the impact of their algorithms on public discourse and to prevent the spread of misinformation and harmful content.

4. Combatting Misinformation: The Tech Accountability Act included provisions to address the spread of misinformation on digital platforms. The law required tech companies to take proactive measures to identify and remove false or misleading content, particularly content related to public health, elections, and national security. It also mandated that companies provide users with accurate information and fact-checking resources to counter misinformation. The law established penalties for companies that failed to take adequate steps to combat misinformation, including fines and restrictions on their content moderation practices.

5. Promoting Competition and Innovation: The Tech Accountability Act aimed to promote competition and innovation in the tech industry by supporting the

development of new and emerging technologies. The law provided funding for research and development in key areas such as artificial intelligence, cybersecurity, and digital infrastructure. It also introduced measures to support startups and small businesses in the tech sector, including access to capital, mentorship programs, and tax incentives. The goal was to create a more dynamic and competitive tech ecosystem that encouraged innovation and reduced the dominance of a few large companies.

The Impact of the Tech Accountability Act

The Tech Accountability Act had a transformative impact on the regulation of the tech industry and the protection of consumers and democracy. By strengthening antitrust enforcement, the law helped to curb the power of tech monopolies and promote competition in the digital marketplace. This, in turn, created more opportunities for innovation and the development of new technologies that benefited consumers.

The data privacy protections introduced by the Tech Accountability Act provided consumers with greater control over their personal information and increased transparency in how their data was used. This helped to restore trust in digital services and reduced the risk of data breaches and misuse of personal information.

The transparency requirements for algorithms and the measures to combat misinformation had a significant impact on the quality of information available on digital platforms.

By holding tech companies accountable for the content and experiences they delivered to users, the law helped to reduce the spread of misinformation and promote more informed public discourse.

However, the implementation of the Tech Accountability Act faced significant challenges. Tech companies pushed back against the new regulations, arguing that they imposed undue burdens on innovation and competitiveness. The law also sparked debates about the balance between government oversight and free expression, particularly in the context of content moderation and misinformation. Despite these challenges, the Tech Accountability Act was widely regarded as a critical step forward in addressing the complex issues posed by the tech industry and ensuring that the digital age was one of progress and accountability.

Balancing Privacy, Security, and Freedom in the Digital Age

As the Harris administration worked to address the challenges of cybersecurity and tech regulation, it also grappled with the broader issue of balancing privacy, security, and freedom in the digital age. The rapid expansion of digital technologies had created new opportunities for innovation and economic growth, but it had also raised important questions about how to protect individual rights and freedoms in a world where data and digital networks played an increasingly central role.

The Digital Bill of Rights

To address these concerns, Harris introduced the Digital Bill of Rights, a comprehensive framework designed to protect the fundamental rights of individuals in the digital age. The Digital Bill of Rights sought to balance the need for security and innovation with the protection of privacy, freedom of expression, and other core democratic values.

The Digital Bill of Rights included several key principles:

1. Right to Privacy: The Digital Bill of Rights affirmed the right of individuals to privacy in their digital lives. This included the right to control how their personal information was collected, used, and shared by tech companies and other entities. The framework established clear guidelines for data privacy, including the requirement for informed consent, the right to access and correct personal data, and the right to have personal data deleted. The Digital Bill of Rights also called for the creation of a federal data protection agency to oversee the enforcement of privacy protections and to hold companies accountable for violations.

2. Right to Freedom of Expression: The Digital Bill of Rights recognized the importance of freedom of expression in the digital age and affirmed the right of individuals to communicate, share information, and express their views online. The framework established protections against censorship and government surveillance, while also recognizing the need to address harmful content and misinformation. The Digital Bill of Rights called for transparency in content moderation practices and established guidelines for ensuring that restrictions on

speech were narrowly tailored and consistent with democratic values.

3. Right to Security: The Digital Bill of Rights affirmed the right of individuals to security in their digital lives. This included the right to be protected from cyberattacks, identity theft, and other forms of digital harm. The framework called for the implementation of strong cybersecurity measures to protect individuals and organizations from digital threats, as well as the development of international norms and agreements to prevent cyber warfare and other forms of state-sponsored cyber aggression.

4. Right to Access and Inclusion: The Digital Bill of Rights recognized the importance of digital access and inclusion in ensuring that all individuals could participate fully in the digital economy and society. The framework called for efforts to close the digital divide by expanding access to high-speed internet, digital devices, and digital literacy programs. It also emphasized the importance of ensuring that digital technologies were accessible to individuals with disabilities and that digital platforms promoted diversity and inclusion.

5. Right to Fairness and Accountability: The Digital Bill of Rights affirmed the right of individuals to fairness and accountability in their interactions with digital technologies. This included the right to be protected from algorithmic bias, discrimination, and unfair treatment. The framework called for transparency in the development and use of

algorithms, as well as the establishment of oversight mechanisms to ensure that digital technologies were used in a fair and equitable manner.

The Impact of the Digital Bill of Rights

The Digital Bill of Rights was a landmark achievement in the effort to protect individual rights and freedoms in the digital age. By establishing clear principles for privacy, security, and freedom of expression, the framework provided a roadmap for navigating the complex challenges of the digital era while safeguarding the core values of democracy.

The right to privacy affirmed by the Digital Bill of Rights had a significant impact on how tech companies and other entities handled personal data. The requirement for informed consent, coupled with the establishment of a federal data protection agency, helped to ensure that individuals had greater control over their digital lives and that their privacy was protected against misuse and exploitation.

The right to freedom of expression provided important protections against censorship and government overreach, while also addressing the challenges of harmful content and misinformation. The emphasis on transparency in content moderation practices helped to build trust in digital platforms and ensured that restrictions on speech were consistent with democratic principles.

The right to security reinforced the importance of strong cybersecurity measures and international cooperation in protecting individuals and organizations from digital threats. The framework's call for fairness and accountability in the use of digital technologies helped to address concerns about algorithmic bias and discrimination, ensuring that digital tools were used in ways that were just and equitable.

While the Digital Bill of Rights was widely praised for its comprehensive approach to protecting individual rights in the digital age, it also faced challenges in implementation. Tech companies and other stakeholders expressed concerns about the potential impact of the framework on innovation and competitiveness, and debates about the balance between privacy, security, and freedom continued to shape the discourse around digital governance.

Despite these challenges, the Digital Bill of Rights was a critical step forward in ensuring that the digital age was one of progress, innovation, and respect for fundamental rights and freedoms.

A Legacy of Innovation and Responsibility

As Kamala Harris's presidency progressed, her administration's efforts to address the challenges of the digital age left a lasting impact on the United States and the world. From strengthening cybersecurity to regulating the tech industry, from promoting innovation to protecting individual rights, Harris's commitment to navigating the complexities of the digital frontier was unwavering.

The initiatives introduced by Harris and her administration helped to create a more secure, accountable, and inclusive digital landscape, one that balanced the needs of innovation and progress with the protection of fundamental rights and freedoms. The National Cybersecurity Initiative, the Tech Accountability Act, and the Digital Bill of Rights all played critical roles in shaping the future of the digital era, ensuring that technology served the public good rather than undermining it.

Harris's leadership in the digital age demonstrated the importance of thoughtful and responsible governance in addressing the challenges of a rapidly evolving world. Her legacy in technology and cybersecurity would be remembered as a time when the United States took bold and decisive action to protect its citizens, promote innovation, and uphold the values of democracy in the face of unprecedented change.

Chapter 13: Military and Defense

A New Vision for Military Strategy

When Kamala Harris assumed the presidency, she inherited a military landscape that was both complex and rapidly evolving. The United States faced a myriad of global security challenges, from the rise of new and sophisticated cyber threats to the enduring presence of overseas conflicts that had stretched on for nearly two decades. Harris, who had long advocated for a more strategic and measured approach to military engagement, was determined to reshape American military policy to meet the demands of the 21st century.

Harris's approach to military strategy was defined by a commitment to modernization, the effective use of cyber warfare capabilities, and a reduction in the United States' involvement in protracted overseas conflicts. She believed that the military needed to adapt to the changing nature of warfare, where traditional combat was increasingly being replaced by digital and asymmetric threats. At the same time, Harris emphasized the importance of supporting veterans and ensuring that those who had served the country received the care and respect they deserved.

Modernizing the U.S. Military: Preparing for the Future

Harris recognized that the U.S. military, while still the most powerful in the world, faced new and emerging challenges that required a fundamental shift in strategy and capabilities. The nature of warfare was changing, with advances in technology and the rise of non-state actors and cyber threats reshaping the battlefield. To maintain its strategic advantage, the U.S. military needed to modernize its forces, invest in new technologies, and adapt to the realities of 21st-century warfare.

The Defense Modernization Initiative

To address these challenges, Harris launched the Defense Modernization Initiative, a comprehensive plan aimed at transforming the U.S. military into a more agile, technologically advanced, and effective force. The initiative focused on several key areas:

1. Investing in Advanced Technologies: The Defense Modernization Initiative placed a strong emphasis on developing and deploying advanced technologies that would give the U.S. military a strategic edge. This included investments in artificial intelligence (AI), autonomous systems, hypersonic weapons, and advanced cyber capabilities. The initiative also prioritized the development of next-generation platforms, such as the B-21 Raider stealth bomber, and the continued modernization of the nuclear triad to ensure the credibility of the U.S. nuclear deterrent.

2. Enhancing Cyber Capabilities: Recognizing that the future of warfare would increasingly be fought in

cyberspace, Harris's initiative prioritized the development of robust cyber capabilities. This included investments in offensive and defensive cyber operations, as well as the integration of cyber warfare into broader military strategy. The initiative also called for the establishment of a Cyber Command with the authority and resources to conduct operations across the spectrum of cyber warfare, from defending critical infrastructure to launching precision cyberattacks against adversaries.

3. Improving Force Readiness and Agility: The Defense Modernization Initiative sought to improve the readiness and agility of U.S. forces, ensuring that they could respond quickly and effectively to emerging threats. This included efforts to streamline command structures, enhance joint operations, and increase the mobility and flexibility of U.S. forces. The initiative also emphasized the importance of maintaining a forward presence in key regions, such as the Indo-Pacific, to deter aggression and reassure allies.

4. Modernizing Military Infrastructure: The initiative included a focus on modernizing military infrastructure, including bases, facilities, and logistics networks. This was critical to ensuring that U.S. forces could operate effectively in a variety of environments and that they had the support they needed to sustain operations. The initiative also included investments in energy resilience and environmental sustainability, recognizing the importance of reducing the military's reliance on fossil fuels and mitigating the impact of climate change on military operations.

5. Strengthening Alliances and Partnerships: Harris's approach to military modernization was not limited to U.S. forces alone; it also emphasized the importance of strengthening alliances and partnerships around the world. The initiative called for increased collaboration with NATO allies, as well as deepening partnerships with key regional players, such as Japan, South Korea, and Australia. This included joint training exercises, intelligence sharing, and coordinated defense planning to enhance collective security and ensure interoperability between U.S. and allied forces.

The Impact of the Defense Modernization Initiative

The Defense Modernization Initiative had a profound impact on the U.S. military's ability to address the challenges of the 21st century. By investing in advanced technologies and enhancing cyber capabilities, the initiative helped to maintain the United States' strategic edge and deter potential adversaries. The integration of AI, autonomous systems, and hypersonic weapons into military operations provided U.S. forces with new and powerful tools to achieve their objectives.

The focus on cyber capabilities was particularly significant, as it allowed the U.S. military to defend critical infrastructure, conduct precision cyber operations, and counter cyberattacks from adversaries. The establishment of a Cyber Command with dedicated resources and authority marked a major step forward in the U.S. military's ability to operate effectively in cyberspace.

The initiative also improved the readiness and agility of U.S. forces, ensuring that they could respond quickly and effectively to emerging threats. The modernization of military infrastructure and the focus on energy resilience and environmental sustainability helped to ensure that U.S. forces could operate effectively in a variety of environments and that they were prepared for the challenges of the future.

However, the Defense Modernization Initiative was not without its challenges. The rapid pace of technological change meant that the U.S. military had to continuously adapt and update its capabilities to stay ahead of adversaries. Additionally, the initiative required significant investments in research and development, which faced scrutiny from lawmakers concerned about the cost of modernization efforts.

Despite these challenges, the Defense Modernization Initiative was widely regarded as a critical achievement of the Harris administration and a key component of the United States' ability to maintain its military superiority in a rapidly changing world.

Cyber Warfare: The New Battlefield

As part of her broader strategy to modernize the U.S. military, Harris placed a strong emphasis on developing and enhancing the nation's cyber warfare capabilities. The rise of cyber threats had fundamentally altered the nature of warfare, with adversaries increasingly using digital tools to target critical infrastructure, steal sensitive information, and disrupt military operations. Harris recognized that the U.S. military needed to be prepared to operate effectively in this new domain and that cyber warfare would play a central role in future conflicts.

The Cyber Warfare Command

One of the key components of Harris's approach to cyber warfare was the establishment of the Cyber Warfare Command, a dedicated branch of the U.S. military focused on conducting cyber operations and defending the nation's digital infrastructure. The Cyber Warfare Command was tasked with a wide range of responsibilities, including offensive and defensive cyber operations, cyber intelligence gathering, and the protection of critical infrastructure from cyberattacks.

The Cyber Warfare Command was structured to operate across the full spectrum of cyber warfare, from tactical operations to strategic-level engagements. This included the ability to launch precision cyberattacks against adversaries, disrupt their command and control networks, and degrade their ability to conduct military operations. The command also worked closely with other branches of the military, as well as with intelligence agencies and civilian government organizations, to coordinate cyber operations and share intelligence.

Offensive Cyber Operations

Harris's administration recognized that to effectively deter cyber threats, the U.S. military needed to have the capability to conduct offensive cyber operations. These operations were designed to target adversaries' digital infrastructure, disrupt their military capabilities, and impose costs on those who sought to harm the United States.

Under the Cyber Warfare Command, the U.S. military developed a range of offensive cyber capabilities, including the ability to conduct cyberattacks against adversaries' critical infrastructure, such as power grids, communication networks, and financial systems. These capabilities were intended to provide the U.S. military with a powerful tool to respond to cyberattacks and to deter adversaries from launching cyber operations against the United States.

Offensive cyber operations were carefully calibrated to avoid escalation and to minimize the risk of unintended consequences. The administration established clear rules of engagement for cyber operations, including the requirement for presidential approval for high-risk or high-impact operations. The goal was to ensure that offensive cyber operations were conducted in a manner consistent with international law and U.S. strategic objectives.

Defensive Cyber Operations

In addition to offensive capabilities, the Cyber Warfare Command also played a critical role in defending the United States from cyber threats. This included the protection of military networks, government systems, and critical infrastructure from cyberattacks, as well as the development of advanced defensive technologies and strategies.

The Cyber Warfare Command worked closely with other government agencies, including the Department of Homeland Security (DHS) and the National Security Agency (NSA), to coordinate defensive efforts and share threat intelligence. The command also collaborated with private sector partners, particularly those in critical industries such as energy, finance, and telecommunications, to enhance the security of their digital infrastructure.

One of the key achievements of the Cyber Warfare Command was the development of advanced threat detection and response capabilities. These capabilities allowed the U.S. military to identify and neutralize cyber threats in real time, preventing potential attacks from causing significant damage. The command also played a key role in developing and implementing cybersecurity best practices across the military and government, ensuring that all branches of the military were prepared to defend against cyber threats.

The Impact of the Cyber Warfare Command

The establishment of the Cyber Warfare Command marked a significant milestone in the U.S. military's ability to operate effectively in the digital domain. By developing and deploying advanced offensive and defensive cyber capabilities, the command provided the U.S. military with a powerful tool to deter adversaries and protect the nation's digital infrastructure.

The Cyber Warfare Command played a critical role in responding to a number of high-profile cyber incidents, including a major cyberattack on U.S. financial institutions in 2026. The command's ability to quickly identify and neutralize the threat helped to prevent widespread disruption and reinforced the importance of maintaining robust cyber capabilities.

The command also played a key role in strengthening the nation's overall cybersecurity posture. Through its collaboration with other government agencies and private sector partners, the command helped to build a more resilient digital infrastructure capable of withstanding sophisticated cyberattacks.

However, the Cyber Warfare Command faced challenges in navigating the complex and rapidly evolving landscape of cyber warfare. The administration had to carefully balance the need for effective cyber operations with the risks of escalation and the potential for unintended consequences. Additionally, the reliance on digital tools and networks created new vulnerabilities that adversaries could exploit, requiring continuous efforts to adapt and strengthen cybersecurity defenses.

Despite these challenges, the Cyber Warfare Command was widely regarded as a critical component of the U.S. military's ability to address the challenges of the digital age and to protect the nation from cyber threats.

A Focus on Strategic Engagement

In place of large-scale, long-term military deployments, Harris's administration pursued a strategy of targeted and strategic engagement. This approach involved the use of special operations forces, precision airstrikes, and intelligence-driven operations to address specific threats without the need for prolonged deployments.

One example of this approach was the administration's strategy in the fight against ISIS and other terrorist groups. Rather than relying on large numbers of ground troops, the U.S. military focused on supporting local partners, conducting targeted airstrikes, and deploying special operations forces to disrupt and dismantle terrorist networks. This approach allowed the United States to maintain pressure on terrorist groups while minimizing the risks and costs associated with large-scale deployments.

The administration also prioritized diplomatic efforts and regional partnerships as key components of its military strategy. Harris believed that addressing the root causes of conflict, such as political instability, economic deprivation, and human rights abuses, required a comprehensive approach that went beyond military force. To this end, the administration worked to strengthen diplomatic engagement, support peace processes, and build the capacity of regional partners to address security challenges.

The Impact of the Shift in Military Engagement

The shift in military engagement under Harris's administration had a significant impact on the United

States' role in global security. By reducing the nation's involvement in protracted conflicts and focusing on targeted and strategic engagement, the administration was able to address specific threats while minimizing the risks and costs associated with large-scale deployments.

The withdrawal from Afghanistan marked a major turning point in U.S. military policy and signaled a broader reevaluation of the nation's approach to military engagement. While the decision to withdraw was not without its challenges and consequences, it reflected Harris's commitment to ending America's "forever wars" and to focusing on more effective and sustainable approaches to global security.

The administration's focus on strategic engagement and regional partnerships also helped to address key security challenges without the need for prolonged military involvement. By supporting local partners, conducting targeted operations, and prioritizing diplomatic efforts, the United States was able to maintain its influence and address threats in a more efficient and effective manner.

However, the shift in military engagement also presented challenges. The reliance on special operations forces and targeted airstrikes raised concerns about the potential for civilian casualties and the long-term effectiveness of such approaches. Additionally, the focus on regional partnerships required careful coordination and support to ensure that local partners had the capacity to address security challenges effectively.

Despite these challenges, the shift in military engagement under Harris's administration was widely regarded as a necessary and strategic adjustment to the realities of modern warfare and global security.

Supporting Veterans and Reforming the Department of Veterans Affairs

In addition to her focus on military strategy and engagement, Harris was deeply committed to supporting veterans and ensuring that those who had served the country received the care and respect they deserved. Throughout her presidency, Harris made it a priority to reform the Department of Veterans Affairs (VA) and to address the challenges facing veterans, including access to healthcare, mental health services, and employment opportunities.

The Veterans Affairs Reform Act

One of the key pieces of legislation championed by Harris was the Veterans Affairs Reform Act, a comprehensive bill aimed at improving the services and support provided to veterans by the VA. The Veterans Affairs Reform Act included several key provisions:

1. Improving Access to Healthcare: The Veterans Affairs Reform Act sought to improve access to healthcare for veterans by expanding the VA's network of healthcare providers and increasing funding for VA medical facilities. The law also included provisions to reduce wait times for appointments, improve the quality of care, and expand

access to specialized services, such as mental health care and treatment for traumatic brain injuries (TBI).

2. Expanding Mental Health Services: Harris recognized that mental health care was a critical need for many veterans, particularly those who had experienced combat-related trauma. The Veterans Affairs Reform Act provided increased funding for mental health services, including the hiring of additional mental health professionals, the expansion of telehealth services, and the development of new programs to address issues such as post-traumatic stress disorder (PTSD) and substance abuse.

3. Supporting Veterans' Employment: The Veterans Affairs Reform Act included provisions to support veterans in their transition to civilian life, particularly in finding employment. The law provided funding for job training programs, apprenticeships, and educational opportunities for veterans. It also established tax credits for employers who hired veterans and expanded support for veteran-owned businesses.

4. Addressing Homelessness Among Veterans: The Veterans Affairs Reform Act included a focus on addressing homelessness among veterans, a persistent issue that had long been a priority for Harris. The law provided funding for housing programs, supportive services, and outreach efforts to help homeless veterans find stable housing and access the care they needed. The law also included initiatives to prevent homelessness among veterans, including rental assistance and eviction prevention programs.

5. Improving Accountability and Transparency: The Veterans Affairs Reform Act introduced new measures to improve accountability and transparency within the VA. This included the establishment of an independent oversight body to monitor the performance of VA facilities and the implementation of new reporting requirements to ensure that veterans received timely and high-quality care. The law also included provisions to protect whistleblowers and to hold VA officials accountable for misconduct or negligence.

The Impact of the Veterans Affairs Reform Act

The Veterans Affairs Reform Act had a significant impact on the services and support provided to veterans by the VA. By improving access to healthcare, expanding mental health services, and supporting veterans in their transition to civilian life, the law helped to address some of the most pressing challenges facing veterans.

The expansion of mental health services was particularly significant, as it provided critical support for veterans struggling with issues such as PTSD and TBI. The increased funding for mental health professionals and the expansion of telehealth services helped to ensure that veterans could access the care they needed, regardless of their location.

The focus on veterans' employment and homelessness also had a positive impact, helping veterans to find stable housing and meaningful employment as they transitioned to civilian life. The job training programs, tax credits, and support for veteran-owned businesses provided veterans with new opportunities to succeed in the civilian workforce.

The improvements in accountability and transparency within the VA helped to restore trust in the agency and ensure that veterans received the care and support they deserved. The independent oversight body and new reporting requirements provided a mechanism for monitoring the performance of VA facilities and holding officials accountable for any shortcomings.

However, the implementation of the Veterans Affairs Reform Act faced challenges, including the need for continued funding and resources to support the expanded services and programs. Additionally, the VA's complex bureaucracy and the scale of the challenges facing veterans required ongoing efforts to ensure that the reforms were fully realized and that veterans received the care and support they needed.

Despite these challenges, the Veterans Affairs Reform Act was widely regarded as a critical achievement of the Harris administration and a key component of the nation's commitment to honoring and supporting those who had served in the military.

The Response to the Rise of China

Another key focus of Harris's military strategy was addressing the rise of China as a global power. The Indo-Pacific region had become a central arena for great power competition, with China's growing military capabilities and assertive actions raising concerns about regional security and the potential for conflict.

Harris's approach to China involved a combination of military deterrence, diplomatic engagement, and the strengthening of alliances and partnerships in the region. The administration prioritized the modernization of U.S. forces in the Indo-Pacific, including the deployment of advanced platforms such as the B-21 Raider and the development of new capabilities for countering anti-access/area denial (A2/AD) strategies.

The administration also worked to strengthen alliances with key regional partners, including Japan, South Korea, and Australia, through joint training exercises, intelligence sharing, and coordinated defense planning. The goal was to maintain a credible deterrent to Chinese aggression while promoting stability and security in the region.

Harris's approach to China also included efforts to manage tensions and prevent conflict through diplomatic engagement. The administration sought to establish channels of communication with Chinese leaders and to engage in dialogue on key issues, such as maritime security, cyber threats, and arms control. While the relationship with China remained complex and often contentious, Harris's strategy aimed to prevent escalation and to find areas of mutual interest where cooperation was possible.

The Fight Against ISIS and Other Terrorist Groups

Another key area of focus for Harris's military strategy was the ongoing fight against ISIS and other terrorist groups. While the territorial defeat of ISIS in Iraq and Syria had been achieved under the previous administration, the group continued to pose a threat through its global network and its ability to inspire lone-wolf attacks.

Harris's approach to counterterrorism involved a combination of targeted military operations, support for local partners, and efforts to address the root causes of terrorism. The administration prioritized the use of special operations forces and precision airstrikes to disrupt and dismantle terrorist networks, while also providing support for local security forces in key regions such as the Middle East and North Africa.

In addition to military efforts, Harris's administration also emphasized the importance of countering violent extremism through non-military means. This included efforts to counter extremist propaganda, promote economic development, and support governance and rule of law in regions vulnerable to terrorist influence.

The impact of Harris's counterterrorism strategy was significant, helping to maintain pressure on terrorist groups and prevent the resurgence of ISIS. However, the fight against terrorism remained an ongoing challenge, requiring continuous efforts to adapt to the evolving threat and to address the underlying factors that fueled extremism.

A Legacy of Strategic Adaptation and Commitment

As Kamala Harris's presidency progressed, her approach to military strategy and defense left a lasting impact on the United States and global security. Her commitment to modernization, the development of cyber warfare capabilities, and the reduction of overseas conflicts reflected a strategic adaptation to the changing nature of warfare and the complexities of the 21st century.

The Defense Modernization Initiative, the establishment of the Cyber Warfare Command, and the decision to withdraw from Afghanistan were all key components of Harris's military strategy, each contributing to the United States' ability to address emerging threats and maintain its global leadership.

Harris's administration also demonstrated a deep commitment to supporting veterans and reforming the Department of Veterans Affairs, ensuring that those who had served the country received the care and respect they deserved.

While the challenges facing the U.S. military and global security were significant, Harris's leadership provided a roadmap for navigating these complexities with strategic foresight and a commitment to the principles of justice, accountability, and global stability. Her legacy in military and defense would be remembered as a time when the United States adapted to the realities of a rapidly changing world and reaffirmed its commitment to protecting its citizens, its allies, and its values.

Chapter 14: The Midterm Elections

The Political Landscape Leading Into the Midterm Elections

As Kamala Harris approached the midpoint of her first term as President, the political landscape was characterized by a mix of optimism, polarization, and uncertainty. The 2026 midterm elections would serve as a crucial test of Harris's leadership and the public's response to her administration's policies. The outcome of these elections would not only determine the balance of power in Congress but also set the stage for the second half of her presidency.

The first two years of Harris's administration had been marked by significant legislative achievements, including the passage of the American Dream Act, the Women's Health Protection Act, the Pay Equity Act, and key defense and cybersecurity initiatives. Additionally, her administration had implemented significant reforms in healthcare, education, and climate policy, reflecting her commitment to progressive change.

However, these accomplishments were set against a backdrop of deep political polarization and ongoing social and economic challenges. The nation remained divided on many of the key issues that Harris had championed, such as immigration, reproductive rights, and environmental policy.

Economic concerns, including inflation and the rising cost of living, continued to weigh heavily on the minds of voters. At the same time, the COVID-19 pandemic, while no longer at its peak, had left lasting impacts on the economy, public health, and social cohesion.

The 2026 midterm elections would be a referendum on Harris's presidency thus far and would provide insight into the electorate's priorities and concerns. For Harris and the Democratic Party, the challenge was to maintain control of both the House of Representatives and the Senate, while also navigating the increasingly polarized political environment.

The Democratic Strategy: Running on Legislative Achievements and Social Justice

As the midterm elections approached, the Democratic Party's strategy centered on highlighting the legislative successes of Harris's first two years in office. The party's message emphasized the administration's efforts to expand access to healthcare, protect reproductive rights, advance gender equality, and address climate change. Democrats also focused on the administration's achievements in modernizing the military, enhancing cybersecurity, and reforming the immigration system.

In addition to these policy accomplishments, the Democratic Party sought to position itself as the defender of democracy and social justice. The party highlighted its efforts to combat voter suppression, protect civil rights, and address systemic racism and inequality. Harris's status as the first woman and the first person of Black and South Asian descent to hold the presidency was also a central theme, as the party sought to mobilize women, people of color, and young voters.

However, the Democrats faced significant challenges in the midterm elections. The historical trend in U.S. politics is that the party of the sitting president often loses seats in Congress during the midterms. This trend, combined with the ongoing polarization of the electorate, made the 2026 midterms particularly challenging for the Democratic Party.

The Republican Strategy: Capitalizing on Economic Concerns and Cultural Issues

The Republican Party, meanwhile, focused its campaign on economic issues and cultural concerns that resonated with its base. Republicans criticized the Harris administration for its handling of the economy, particularly with regard to inflation and the rising cost of living. They argued that the administration's policies, including increased government spending and regulations, had contributed to economic instability and hurt working families.

Republicans also sought to capitalize on cultural and social issues, which had become increasingly salient in the political discourse. The party's messaging emphasized opposition to what it characterized as "radical" progressive policies, including the administration's stance on immigration, criminal justice reform, and gender and sexual orientation issues. Republicans framed these issues as part of a broader cultural battle, positioning themselves as defenders of traditional values and individual freedoms.

The Republican strategy aimed to energize its base and appeal to swing voters who were concerned about the economy, national security, and cultural issues. However, the party also faced internal divisions, particularly between the more traditional establishment wing and the populist wing that had gained influence in recent years.

The Battle for Control of Congress

The stakes in the 2026 midterm elections were high, as control of both the House of Representatives and the Senate hung in the balance. Democrats entered the midterms with a narrow majority in both chambers, but the margins were slim, and several key races were highly competitive.

In the House, Democrats held a slight majority, but the party faced a challenging map, with several vulnerable incumbents in swing districts. Republicans focused their efforts on flipping these districts, targeting areas where Harris's policies were less popular or where economic concerns were particularly acute. Democrats, meanwhile, sought to defend their incumbents by emphasizing the benefits of the administration's policies and mobilizing key constituencies, including women, people of color, and young voters.

The Senate, the split was 50/50, was a major battleground in the midterms. Several key Senate races were closely contested, with both parties pouring significant resources into these races. Republicans aimed to flip enough seats to regain control of the Senate, while Democrats focused on defending their incumbents and potentially expanding their majority by winning in traditionally Republican states.

Voter Sentiment: The Mood of the Electorate

As the midterm elections approached, voter sentiment was characterized by a mix of optimism, frustration, and anxiety. Polling data indicated that the electorate was deeply divided, with significant variation in how different demographic groups viewed the Harris administration and the state of the country.

For many Democratic voters, particularly women, people of color, and young voters, the first two years of Harris's presidency were seen as a period of significant progress on issues such as healthcare, gender equality, and climate change. These voters were generally supportive of the administration's policies and were motivated to turn out in the midterms to defend and expand the Democratic majorities in Congress.

However, economic concerns loomed large for many voters, particularly those in swing districts and traditionally Republican areas. Rising inflation, the cost of living, and concerns about job security were major issues for these voters, who were more likely to view the administration's economic policies as contributing to these challenges. For these voters, the midterms represented an opportunity to express their dissatisfaction with the direction of the economy and to push for a change in leadership.

Cultural and social issues also played a significant role in shaping voter sentiment. The Republican base, energized by concerns about immigration, crime, and what they perceived as "radical" progressive policies, was highly motivated to turn out in the midterms. These voters were generally critical of the Harris administration and viewed the midterms as a chance to push back against the administration's agenda.

The electorate's mood was further influenced by the lingering effects of the COVID-19 pandemic. While the immediate crisis had passed, the pandemic had left lasting impacts on public health, the economy, and social cohesion. Voters were concerned about the long-term consequences of the pandemic and how the government would address these challenges moving forward.

The Midterm Election Results: A Mixed Verdict

The 2026 midterm elections produced a mixed verdict, reflecting the deep divisions within the electorate and the complex political landscape. While both parties experienced gains and losses, the overall outcome of the elections had significant implications for the remainder of Harris's term.

In the House of Representatives, Republicans were able to make gains, flipping several swing districts and narrowing the Democratic majority. However, Democrats managed to retain control of the House, albeit with a reduced margin. The results in the House reflected the challenges that

Democrats faced in defending their incumbents in competitive districts, as well as the effectiveness of the Republican strategy in appealing to voters concerned about the economy and cultural issues.

The Senate results were even more closely contested, with several key races coming down to the wire. In the end, Democrats were able to control of the Senate, but by the narrowest of margins. The outcome in the Senate was seen as a significant victory for Harris and the Democratic Party, as it allowed them to continue advancing their legislative agenda and confirming judicial appointments without Republican obstruction.

The mixed results of the midterm elections had important implications for the remainder of Harris's term. While Democrats retained control of both chambers of Congress, the reduced majorities made it more difficult to pass ambitious legislation and required greater efforts to build consensus within the party and across the aisle.

The Challenges of Governing in a Polarized Environment

The 2026 midterm elections underscored the challenges of governing in a deeply polarized environment. The results reflected the sharp divisions within the electorate, with voters increasingly aligning along partisan, ideological, and cultural lines. For Harris, navigating this polarized landscape would require a delicate balance between advancing her administration's priorities and addressing the concerns of a diverse and divided electorate.

One of the key challenges facing Harris in the aftermath of the midterms was the need to build coalitions and find common ground, both within her party and with Republicans. With narrower majorities in Congress, Harris and Democratic leaders had to work to unite their caucus and bring together different factions of the party, including progressives and moderates, to pass legislation.

At the same time, Harris recognized the importance of engaging with Republicans and seeking bipartisan support for key initiatives. While the polarization of the political environment made bipartisan cooperation more difficult, Harris believed that finding areas of agreement was essential for governing effectively and addressing the nation's most pressing challenges.

The polarization of the electorate also posed challenges for Harris's efforts to communicate with the public and build support for her policies. In an environment where misinformation and partisan media played a significant role in shaping public opinion, Harris and her administration had to work to cut through the noise and reach voters with a clear and compelling message.

Despite these challenges, Harris remained committed to her vision for the country and to the principles that had guided her presidency thus far. She continued to prioritize issues such as healthcare, climate change, gender equality, and social justice, while also addressing the economic concerns that had played a significant role in the midterm elections.

MADAM PRESIDENT: THE FIRST TERM OF KAMALA HARRIS

The Path Forward

As Kamala Harris entered the second half of her first term, the results of the 2026 midterm elections provided both opportunities and challenges. The mixed verdict of the electorate reflected the complexity of the political landscape and the deep divisions within the country. For Harris, the path forward required a careful balance between advancing her administration's priorities and addressing the concerns of a diverse and divided electorate.

The reduced majorities in Congress meant that Harris would need to work harder to build coalitions and find common ground, both within her party and across the aisle. The challenges of governing in a polarized environment required a focus on communication, consensus-building, and strategic engagement.

Despite the difficulties, Harris remained committed to her vision for the country and to the principles that had guided her presidency thus far. The midterm elections served as a reminder of the importance of perseverance, adaptability, and leadership in the face of uncertainty. As Harris looked ahead to the remainder of her term, she remained determined to continue working toward a more just, equitable, and prosperous future for all Americans.

Chapter 15: Tackling Economic Inequality

A Commitment to Reducing Economic Inequality

Economic inequality had been a central issue in American politics for decades, but by the time Kamala Harris assumed the presidency, it had reached levels not seen since the early 20th century. The wealth gap between the richest Americans and everyone else had widened dramatically, exacerbated by factors such as the rise of technology, globalization, and tax policies that disproportionately benefited the wealthy. For millions of Americans, the promise of the American Dream—where hard work and perseverance could lead to a better life—seemed increasingly out of reach.

President Harris recognized that reducing economic inequality was not only a matter of social justice but also essential for the long-term stability and prosperity of the country. She understood that extreme inequality undermined the fabric of society, leading to political polarization, social unrest, and a loss of trust in institutions. As such, tackling economic inequality became one of the defining missions of her administration.

Harris's approach to reducing economic inequality was multifaceted, involving a range of policies aimed at reforming the tax system, raising wages, expanding social welfare programs, and addressing the structural barriers that kept many Americans from achieving economic security.

Tax Reform: Creating a Fairer System

One of the central pillars of Harris's strategy to reduce economic inequality was tax reform. The U.S. tax system, while progressive on paper, had increasingly come under criticism for allowing the wealthiest individuals and corporations to pay far less than their fair share. Loopholes, deductions, and preferential treatment for capital gains and dividends had created a system where the rich could amass and protect their wealth, while working- and middle-class Americans faced a heavier burden.

The Fair Share Tax Act

To address these disparities, Harris introduced the Fair Share Tax Act, a comprehensive tax reform bill aimed at ensuring that the wealthiest Americans and corporations paid their fair share of taxes. The Fair Share Tax Act included several key provisions:

1. Raising Taxes on the Wealthiest: The Fair Share Tax Act increased income tax rates for the top 1% of earners, reversing some of the tax cuts that had been implemented under previous administrations. The new top marginal tax rate was set at 39.6%, up from 37%, with an additional surtax on incomes over $10 million. The goal was to ensure that those who benefited the most from the economy contributed proportionally to its upkeep.

2. Closing Loopholes: The act targeted a range of tax loopholes that had allowed the wealthy to minimize their tax liabilities. This included closing the carried interest loophole, which allowed hedge fund managers and private equity investors to pay lower tax rates on their earnings, and eliminating the step-up in basis for inherited assets, which allowed wealthy individuals to pass on large amounts of wealth tax-free.

3. Increasing Capital Gains Taxes: The Fair Share Tax Act also raised the tax rate on capital gains and dividends for high-income individuals, aligning these rates more closely with the rates on ordinary income. Harris argued that income from investments should be taxed at the same rate as income from labor, and that the current system disproportionately benefited those who were already wealthy.

4. Corporate Tax Reform: The Fair Share Tax Act included significant changes to the corporate tax code, including raising the corporate tax rate to 28%, up from the 21% set by the previous administration. The act also introduced a minimum tax on corporate profits to ensure that large corporations, particularly those that had used loopholes to avoid paying taxes, contributed to federal revenue. Additionally, the act sought to crack down on profit shifting and other practices used by multinational corporations to avoid paying U.S. taxes.

5. Expanding the Earned Income Tax Credit (EITC): To support low- and middle-income workers, the Fair Share

Tax Act expanded the Earned Income Tax Credit (EITC), increasing the maximum credit and broadening eligibility. This provision was designed to provide additional financial support to working families and to reduce the tax burden on those earning lower wages.

The Impact of the Fair Share Tax Act

The Fair Share Tax Act was a significant achievement for the Harris administration and had a profound impact on the distribution of wealth and income in the United States. By raising taxes on the wealthiest individuals and corporations, the act generated substantial revenue that could be used to fund social welfare programs, infrastructure projects, and other initiatives aimed at reducing inequality.

The changes to the corporate tax code and the increase in capital gains taxes also contributed to a more equitable tax system, where income from wealth was taxed more similarly to income from labor. This helped to address the growing concentration of wealth at the top and ensured that the benefits of economic growth were more widely shared.

The expansion of the EITC provided immediate financial relief to millions of low- and middle-income workers, helping to lift many out of poverty and reduce the economic stress on working families. By putting more money in the pockets of those who needed it most, the act also helped to stimulate consumer spending and support economic growth.

However, the Fair Share Tax Act faced significant opposition, particularly from Republicans and business interests who argued that the tax increases would stifle economic growth, discourage investment, and lead to job losses. Critics also warned that raising corporate taxes could drive businesses overseas, reducing the competitiveness of the U.S. economy.

Despite these criticisms, the Fair Share Tax Act was widely regarded as a critical step toward creating a more just and equitable tax system. The additional revenue generated by the act allowed the Harris administration to fund a range of programs aimed at reducing economic inequality and improving the lives of ordinary Americans.

Raising Wages: Ensuring Economic Security for All

In addition to tax reform, Harris's administration prioritized efforts to raise wages and ensure that all workers could earn a living wage. Despite the economic growth of recent decades, wages for many workers had stagnated, and millions of Americans continued to struggle with low pay, job insecurity, and the rising cost of living.

The Raise the Wage Act

One of the key initiatives aimed at addressing wage stagnation was the Raise the Wage Act, which sought to increase the federal minimum wage to $15 per hour over a five-year period. Harris had long been a supporter of a higher minimum wage, arguing that no one working full-time should live in poverty. The Raise the Wage Act was designed to lift millions of workers out of poverty, reduce income inequality, and stimulate economic growth by increasing the purchasing power of low-wage workers.

The Raise the Wage Act included several key provisions:

1. Gradual Increase to $15: The act proposed a gradual increase in the federal minimum wage, starting with an immediate increase to $9.50 per hour, followed by incremental increases over the next five years until it reached $15 per hour. After reaching $15, the minimum wage would be indexed to median wage growth, ensuring that it kept pace with inflation and the cost of living.

2. Eliminating the Tipped Minimum Wage: The Raise the Wage Act also included a provision to eliminate the tipped minimum wage, which allowed employers to pay tipped workers, such as servers and bartenders, a lower base wage, relying on tips to make up the difference. The act proposed raising the tipped minimum wage to match the regular minimum wage, ensuring that all workers received a fair and stable income. This act also saw taxes on tipped income decrease.

3. Supporting Small Businesses: To address concerns about the impact of a higher minimum wage on small businesses, the Raise the Wage Act included provisions to support small employers, including tax credits and access to low-interest loans. These measures were designed to help small businesses manage the transition to a higher wage floor and to mitigate any potential negative impacts on employment.

The Impact of the Raise the Wage Act

The Raise the Wage Act had a significant impact on the lives of millions of American workers, particularly those in low-wage jobs. The gradual increase in the federal minimum wage provided a substantial boost to the incomes of workers who had struggled to make ends meet on low pay. For many, the additional income meant greater financial security, the ability to afford basic necessities, and the opportunity to save for the future.

The elimination of the tipped minimum wage was also a major victory for workers in the service industry, many of whom had long faced economic uncertainty due to the reliance on tips. By ensuring that all workers received a stable and fair wage, the act helped to reduce economic vulnerability and promote greater equality in the labor market.

The impact of the Raise the Wage Act was particularly pronounced in regions where the cost of living was high and wages had remained stagnant. In cities like New York, Los Angeles, and San Francisco, the increase in the minimum wage helped to alleviate some of the financial pressures on low-wage workers, making it easier for them to afford housing, healthcare, and other essential expenses.

However, the Raise the Wage Act also faced criticism and opposition, particularly from business groups and conservative lawmakers. Critics argued that raising the minimum wage would lead to job losses, particularly in industries such as retail, hospitality, and food service, where profit margins were slim. They warned that businesses, particularly small businesses, would be forced to cut jobs, reduce hours, or raise prices to offset the higher labor costs.

In response to these concerns, the Harris administration pointed to studies and evidence suggesting that the benefits of raising the minimum wage outweighed the potential drawbacks. Research indicated that higher wages could lead to increased productivity, reduced employee turnover, and higher consumer spending, all of which could contribute to economic growth.

Despite the debates, the Raise the Wage Act was widely seen as a critical step toward reducing economic inequality and ensuring that all workers could earn a living wage. The act was a key component of Harris's broader strategy to create an economy that worked for everyone, not just the wealthy.

Expanding Social Welfare Programs: Building a Stronger Safety Net

Another major focus of Harris's administration in reducing economic inequality was the expansion of social welfare programs. Harris believed that a strong social safety net was essential for ensuring that all Americans had access to basic needs such as healthcare, housing, education, and food security. She also saw social welfare programs as a way to address the structural barriers that kept many people in poverty, such as lack of access to affordable childcare, healthcare, and education.

The Social Equity and Opportunity Act

To address these issues, Harris introduced the Social Equity and Opportunity Act, a comprehensive bill aimed at expanding and strengthening social welfare programs to reduce poverty and economic inequality. The Social Equity and Opportunity Act included several key provisions:

1. Universal Childcare and Pre-K: One of the centerpiece initiatives of the act was the creation of a universal childcare and pre-K program, designed to provide affordable, high-quality early childhood education and care to all families. The program aimed to support working parents, particularly women, by reducing the burden of childcare costs and ensuring that all children had access to the early education they needed to succeed in school and life.

2. Expanding Healthcare Access: The Social Equity and Opportunity Act included provisions to expand access to healthcare, particularly for low-income individuals and families. The act expanded Medicaid eligibility, increased subsidies for health insurance under the Affordable Care Act, and introduced a public option to provide an affordable alternative to private insurance. The goal was to ensure that all Americans had access to quality healthcare, regardless of their income or employment status.

3. Affordable Housing Initiatives: The act also included measures to address the growing affordable housing crisis, particularly in urban areas where housing costs had skyrocketed. The act provided funding for the construction

of affordable housing units, expanded rental assistance programs, and introduced measures to prevent evictions and homelessness. The goal was to ensure that all Americans had access to safe and affordable housing.

4. Expanding SNAP and Nutrition Programs: The Social Equity and Opportunity Act expanded the Supplemental Nutrition Assistance Program (SNAP) and other nutrition programs to ensure that all Americans had access to healthy and affordable food. The act increased benefits for SNAP recipients, expanded eligibility, and provided funding for programs that promoted healthy eating and nutrition education.

5. Support for Education and Job Training: The act included provisions to expand access to education and job training programs, particularly for low-income individuals and those facing barriers to employment. This included funding for community colleges, vocational training programs, and apprenticeships, as well as initiatives to support adult education and literacy programs. The goal was to provide individuals with the skills and education they needed to secure good-paying jobs and achieve economic mobility.

The Impact of the Social Equity and Opportunity Act

The Social Equity and Opportunity Act had a transformative impact on the lives of millions of Americans, particularly those who had struggled with poverty and economic insecurity. By expanding access to affordable childcare, healthcare, housing, and nutrition, the act helped to reduce the economic stress on families and provided a stronger safety net for those in need.

The universal childcare and pre-K program was particularly impactful, providing parents with the support they needed to balance work and family responsibilities. The program also had long-term benefits for children, who received high-quality early education that set them on a path to success in school and life.

The expansion of healthcare access under the act helped to reduce the number of uninsured Americans and provided critical support to low-income individuals and families. The introduction of a public option provided an affordable alternative to private insurance, helping to lower healthcare costs and increase access to care.

The affordable housing initiatives included in the act also had a significant impact, particularly in urban areas where housing costs had become prohibitively expensive. The construction of affordable housing units, combined with expanded rental assistance and eviction prevention programs, helped to reduce homelessness and provide stable housing for families in need.

The expansion of SNAP and other nutrition programs provided critical support to those facing food insecurity, ensuring that all Americans had access to healthy and affordable food. The increased benefits and expanded eligibility helped to reduce hunger and improve nutrition outcomes for low-income families.

However, the Social Equity and Opportunity Act faced challenges and opposition, particularly from those who argued that the expansion of social welfare programs would lead to increased government spending and higher taxes. Critics also warned that the act could create disincentives for work and lead to greater dependency on government assistance.

In response, the Harris administration emphasized the importance of social welfare programs in reducing poverty and inequality, and argued that the investments made under the act would pay off in the long term by creating a healthier, more educated, and more productive workforce.

The Debate Around Capitalism, Socialism, and the Role of Government in the Economy

As Harris's administration implemented its ambitious agenda to reduce economic inequality, the broader debate around capitalism, socialism, and the role of government in the economy intensified. The policies pursued by Harris were seen by some as a necessary response to the excesses of capitalism and the growing concentration of wealth and power. Others, however, viewed these policies as a step toward socialism and a dangerous expansion of government control over the economy.

The Case for Progressive Capitalism

Harris and her administration positioned their approach as one of "progressive capitalism," where the government played an active role in regulating markets, ensuring fair competition, and providing a robust social safety net, while still maintaining a market-based economy. Harris argued that capitalism had the potential to create prosperity and innovation, but that it needed to be balanced with strong regulations and social programs to ensure that the benefits of economic growth were widely shared.

Harris's vision of progressive capitalism was rooted in the belief that economic inequality was not only a moral issue but also a threat to the long-term stability of the economy. She argued that when wealth and power were concentrated in the hands of a few, it undermined democracy, stifled innovation, and limited opportunities for ordinary people. By addressing economic inequality, Harris believed that her administration could create a more dynamic, inclusive, and sustainable economy.

The Critique of Socialism

Critics of Harris's policies, particularly those on the right, argued that her administration's approach was a step toward socialism and a threat to individual freedom and economic growth. They contended that the expansion of government programs, the increase in taxes, and the regulation of markets would stifle entrepreneurship, discourage investment, and lead to inefficiencies in the economy.

These critics warned that Harris's policies would create a culture of dependency, where individuals and businesses relied on government support rather than innovation and hard work. They also expressed concerns about the long-term sustainability of the expanded social welfare programs, arguing that they would lead to higher deficits and debt, burdening future generations.

The Role of Government in the Economy

The debate over the role of government in the economy was not new, but it took on renewed significance during Harris's presidency. The administration's efforts to reduce economic inequality through tax reform, wage increases, and social welfare programs highlighted the tension between the belief in free markets and the need for government intervention to address market failures and social injustices.

Harris and her supporters argued that government intervention was necessary to correct the excesses of capitalism and to ensure that the economy worked for everyone, not just the wealthy. They pointed to the success of social democracies in Europe, where strong social safety nets, progressive taxation, and robust regulations had led to lower levels of inequality, higher levels of social mobility, and greater overall well-being.

Opponents, however, maintained that the best way to reduce inequality and promote prosperity was through limited government intervention and the promotion of free markets. They argued that policies that promoted economic growth, entrepreneurship, and innovation were the most effective ways to create jobs, raise wages, and improve living standards for all Americans.

The Impact of the Debate on Public Opinion and Policy

The debate around capitalism, socialism, and the role of government in the economy had a significant impact on public opinion and the political landscape during Harris's presidency. The policies pursued by the administration were popular among progressives and many Democrats, who saw them as necessary steps to address the growing inequality and economic insecurity faced by many Americans.

However, the debate also fueled polarization and division, particularly along partisan lines. Republicans and conservatives were generally opposed to Harris's policies, viewing them as an overreach of government power and a threat to economic freedom. This polarization made it difficult to achieve bipartisan support for many of the administration's initiatives, leading to contentious battles in Congress.

Despite the challenges, Harris remained committed to her vision of progressive capitalism and continued to advocate for policies that promoted economic fairness, social justice, and shared prosperity. She believed that by addressing economic inequality and creating a more inclusive economy, her administration could lay the foundation for a stronger, more resilient, and more equitable society.

A Legacy of Economic Justice

As Kamala Harris's presidency progressed, her administration's efforts to tackle economic inequality left a lasting impact on the United States. Through tax reforms, wage increases, and the expansion of social welfare programs, Harris worked to create a more just and equitable economy, where all Americans had the opportunity to succeed.

The Fair Share Tax Act, the Raise the Wage Act, and the Social Equity and Opportunity Act were key components of Harris's strategy to reduce inequality and improve the lives of ordinary Americans. These initiatives helped to create a fairer tax system, ensure that all workers earned a living wage, and provide a stronger safety net for those in need.

The debate around capitalism, socialism, and the role of government in the economy highlighted the challenges of governing in a polarized environment, but it also underscored the importance of addressing the deep-seated issues that had contributed to growing inequality and economic insecurity.

As Harris looked ahead to the remainder of her term, she remained committed to her vision of progressive capitalism and continued to work toward a more just, inclusive, and prosperous society. Her legacy in tackling economic inequality would be remembered as a time when the United States took bold steps to address the challenges of the 21st century and to create an economy that worked for everyone.

Chapter 16: Crisis and Leadership

A **Sudden Crisis: The Global Economic Downturn of 2027**

As the year 2027 dawned, Kamala Harris was preparing to build on the accomplishments of her first two years in office. With significant legislative victories in healthcare, education, climate change, and economic reform, her administration was eager to press forward with its agenda. However, just as the country seemed to be finding its footing, a sudden and severe global economic downturn tested Harris's leadership in ways she could never have anticipated.

The crisis began with a series of economic shocks that reverberated around the world. Key markets in Asia and Europe experienced sharp contractions due to a combination of geopolitical tensions, supply chain disruptions, and a dramatic drop in consumer confidence. These shocks were further exacerbated by a significant spike in global energy prices, driven by an unexpected series of natural disasters that disrupted oil and gas production in key regions. As the effects of these events rippled through the global economy, the United States found itself at the epicenter of a rapidly unfolding economic crisis.

The economic downturn quickly manifested in the U.S. as financial markets plummeted, corporate earnings declined sharply, and unemployment began to rise. Within weeks, it became clear that the country was facing its most severe economic challenge since the Great Recession of 2008, with the potential to surpass even that crisis in its scope and impact.

For President Harris, the crisis was both a daunting challenge and an opportunity to demonstrate her leadership. As the nation looked to the White House for direction, Harris and her administration had to navigate a complex and rapidly evolving situation that demanded swift, decisive, and effective action.

The Administration's Response: A Comprehensive Strategy

From the outset of the crisis, Harris made it clear that her administration would respond with a comprehensive strategy aimed at stabilizing the economy, protecting American workers, and ensuring that the country emerged from the downturn stronger and more resilient. To that end, she convened her economic team, including Treasury Secretary Elizabeth Warren, Federal Reserve Chair Lael Brainard, and National Economic Council Director Cecilia Rouse, to develop and implement a coordinated response.

The administration's strategy focused on three key areas: stabilizing financial markets, supporting workers and businesses, and addressing the underlying causes of the downturn.

Stabilizing Financial Markets

One of the administration's first priorities was to stabilize the financial markets, which had been sent into a tailspin by the global economic shocks. To restore confidence and prevent further declines, the Federal Reserve took immediate action by cutting interest rates and implementing a new round of quantitative easing. These measures were aimed at increasing liquidity in the financial system, lowering borrowing costs, and encouraging investment.

At the same time, Harris's administration worked closely with Congress to pass the Financial Stability and Resilience Act, a sweeping piece of legislation designed to provide emergency support to the financial sector while also implementing new safeguards to prevent future crises. The act included provisions to strengthen oversight of major financial institutions, increase transparency in financial markets, and enhance protections for consumers and investors.

To further stabilize the financial system, the administration also established the Market Recovery Fund, a $500 billion fund aimed at supporting key sectors of the economy that had been hardest hit by the downturn, including energy, technology, and manufacturing. The fund provided targeted financial assistance to companies in these sectors, helping to prevent widespread bankruptcies and layoffs.

Supporting Workers and Businesses

While stabilizing the financial markets was critical, Harris understood that the true measure of the administration's response would be its ability to protect American workers and businesses from the worst effects of the downturn. To that end, the administration launched a series of initiatives aimed at providing direct support to those most affected by the crisis.

One of the centerpiece initiatives was the Economic Security and Recovery Act, which included a range of measures to provide immediate financial relief to workers and businesses. The act expanded unemployment benefits, including extending the duration of benefits and increasing the weekly payment amounts. It also provided direct cash payments to individuals and families, similar to the stimulus checks distributed during the COVID-19 pandemic, to help Americans cover essential expenses during the downturn. This would be the basis for Harris's Universal Basic Income initiative in her second term.

For businesses, the act included provisions to support small and medium-sized enterprises (SMEs), which were particularly vulnerable to the economic shock. The act established the Small Business Recovery Program, which provided forgivable loans and grants to SMEs to help them weather the crisis, retain employees, and stay afloat. The program also offered targeted support for minority-owned and women-owned businesses, recognizing the disproportionate impact of the downturn on these communities.

In addition to these measures, the administration launched a major infrastructure investment program, the American

Renewal Initiative, aimed at creating jobs and stimulating economic growth. The initiative included funding for a wide range of projects, including the modernization of transportation networks, the expansion of broadband access, and the development of green energy infrastructure. By investing in these critical areas, the administration sought to provide immediate economic stimulus while also laying the groundwork for long-term growth and resilience.

Addressing the Underlying Causes

While the immediate focus of the administration's response was on stabilizing the economy and providing relief, Harris was determined to address the underlying causes of the downturn to prevent a similar crisis from occurring in the future. To that end, her administration pursued a series of structural reforms aimed at addressing the vulnerabilities that had been exposed by the crisis.

One of the key areas of focus was global supply chains, which had been severely disrupted by the economic shocks and natural disasters. The administration launched the Resilient Supply Chains Initiative, a comprehensive effort to strengthen and diversify the nation's supply chains. This initiative included incentives for companies to bring manufacturing back to the United States, as well as investments in technology and infrastructure to enhance the resilience of critical supply chains.

The administration also took steps to address the energy price shocks that had contributed to the downturn. Harris's administration accelerated its efforts to transition the country to renewable energy sources, reducing reliance on fossil fuels and increasing the resilience of the energy sector. The administration expanded investments in solar, wind, and battery storage technologies, while also promoting energy efficiency and conservation.

Finally, the administration pursued reforms to the international financial system, working with global partners to strengthen financial regulations, enhance transparency, and improve coordination in response to future crises. Harris believed that a more stable and equitable global financial system was essential for preventing future downturns and ensuring long-term economic stability.

The Public's Reaction: Resilience and Division

The public's reaction to the crisis and the administration's response was mixed, reflecting the deep divisions within the country and the varying impacts of the downturn on different communities.

For many Americans, particularly those who were directly affected by the economic downturn, the administration's response was a lifeline. The expansion of unemployment benefits, direct cash payments, and support for small businesses provided critical relief during a time of uncertainty and fear. The infrastructure investment program created new job opportunities and helped to stimulate local economies, providing hope for a brighter future.

Polls showed that a majority of Americans supported the administration's efforts to stabilize the economy and provide relief, with many viewing Harris's leadership during the crisis as decisive and effective. Her approval ratings, which had been strong before the crisis, remained solid, with most Americans expressing confidence in her ability to navigate the country through the downturn.

However, the crisis also exacerbated existing political and social divisions, with some Americans expressing skepticism or outright opposition to the administration's approach. Critics, particularly those on the right, argued that the administration's response represented an overreach of government power and would lead to higher taxes, increased debt, and greater government control over the economy.

Some business leaders and conservative lawmakers expressed concerns about the impact of the administration's policies on free markets and economic growth, warning that the expanded role of government in the economy could stifle innovation and competition. These critics also raised concerns about the long-term sustainability of the government's spending programs, arguing that they would lead to higher deficits and debt, burdening future generations.

The debate over the administration's response to the crisis played out in the media and in Congress, with partisan divisions becoming more pronounced. While Democrats generally supported the administration's approach, Republicans were more divided, with some advocating for a more limited government response and others expressing support for targeted relief measures.

The crisis also had a profound impact on public discourse, with many Americans grappling with questions about the future of the economy, the role of government, and the nature of capitalism itself. The downturn brought to the forefront issues of economic inequality, corporate responsibility, and the need for a more resilient and sustainable economic system.

Shaping the Remainder of Harris's Term: A Renewed Focus on Economic Resilience

As the country began to emerge from the depths of the economic downturn, the experience of the crisis had a profound impact on the remainder of Harris's term and her approach to governance. The crisis underscored the importance of economic resilience, both in terms of preventing future downturns and in ensuring that the economy worked for all Americans.

One of the key lessons that Harris drew from the crisis was the need for a more proactive and preventive approach to economic policy. She recognized that the vulnerabilities exposed by the downturn—whether in global supply chains, the energy sector, or the financial system—needed to be addressed through long-term structural reforms. As such, her administration doubled down on efforts to build a more resilient and inclusive economy.

Building Economic Resilience

To build economic resilience, Harris's administration pursued a range of initiatives aimed at strengthening the foundations of the U.S. economy and reducing its vulnerability to future shocks.

Investing in Infrastructure and Technology

The American Renewal Initiative, which had been launched during the crisis, became a central focus of the administration's efforts to build economic resilience. The initiative was expanded to include additional investments in infrastructure and technology, with a focus on projects that would enhance the country's ability to withstand future economic shocks.

Key areas of investment included the modernization of transportation networks, the expansion of broadband access to rural and underserved communities, and the development of smart grid technologies to enhance the resilience of the energy sector. The administration also invested in research and development for emerging technologies, such as artificial intelligence, quantum computing, and advanced manufacturing, to position the United States as a leader in the industries of the future.

Strengthening Social Safety Nets

The crisis also reinforced the importance of strong social safety nets in protecting individuals and families from economic hardship. In response, Harris's administration worked to expand and strengthen social welfare programs, including unemployment insurance, healthcare, and food assistance.

The administration introduced the Economic Security Act, which aimed to make permanent many of the temporary measures implemented during the crisis, such as expanded unemployment benefits and increased funding for SNAP and other nutrition programs. The act also included provisions to strengthen the social safety net for gig workers, freelancers, and other non-traditional workers who had been particularly vulnerable during the downturn.

Promoting Economic Justice

The experience of the crisis also deepened Harris's commitment to promoting economic justice and addressing the structural inequalities that had contributed to the severity of the downturn. The administration continued to pursue policies aimed at reducing economic inequality, including tax reform, wage increases, and support for minority-owned businesses.

Harris also launched the Inclusive Economy Initiative, a comprehensive effort to promote economic opportunities for historically marginalized communities. The initiative included funding for education and job training programs, support for entrepreneurship and small business development, and efforts to close the racial wealth gap.

Strengthening Global Partnerships

The global nature of the economic downturn highlighted the interconnectedness of the world economy and the importance of international cooperation in addressing economic challenges. In response, Harris's administration worked to strengthen global partnerships and promote a more stable and equitable international economic system.

Harris took a leading role in efforts to reform global financial institutions, such as the International Monetary Fund (IMF) and the World Bank, to ensure that they were better equipped to respond to future crises and to support sustainable development. The administration also worked with key allies to strengthen global supply chains, promote fair trade practices, and address global challenges such as climate change and pandemics.

The Legacy of Crisis Leadership

The global economic downturn of 2027 was a defining moment of Harris's presidency, testing her leadership and the resilience of the country. The crisis forced Harris and her administration to respond to a rapidly evolving situation with swift and decisive action, while also grappling with the long-term implications for the economy and society.

Harris's leadership during the crisis was widely praised for its effectiveness, particularly in stabilizing the economy, providing relief to those most affected, and laying the groundwork for long-term recovery. Her administration's response was seen as a model of crisis management, combining immediate action with a focus on structural reforms to prevent future downturns.

The experience of the crisis also shaped Harris's legacy as a leader committed to economic justice and resilience. Her administration's efforts to address the root causes of the downturn, promote economic opportunities for all Americans, and strengthen global partnerships were seen as critical steps toward creating a more inclusive and sustainable economy.

As Harris looked ahead to the remainder of her term, the lessons of the crisis continued to inform her approach to governance. The experience reinforced her belief in the importance of proactive and preventive economic policy, as well as the need for strong social safety nets and a commitment to economic justice.

The global economic downturn of 2027 would be remembered as one of the most significant challenges of Harris's presidency, but it would also be seen as a moment when her leadership helped to guide the country through a time of uncertainty and fear, and set it on a path toward a stronger and more resilient future.

Chapter 17: Judicial Appointments and Legal Battles

Shaping the Federal Judiciary: Harris's Impact on the Courts

One of the most enduring legacies of any U.S. president is the influence they have on the federal judiciary. Judges and justices, particularly those appointed to lifetime positions on the Supreme Court and other federal courts, can shape the interpretation of law for decades, long after a president's term has ended. For President Kamala Harris, the opportunity to appoint judges was not just a chance to leave her mark on the legal landscape; it was an essential part of her broader vision for social justice, equality, and the rule of law.

Harris came into office with a clear understanding of the importance of the judiciary in shaping American society. As a former prosecutor, Attorney General of California, and U.S. Senator, she had seen firsthand how the courts could both protect and challenge the rights of individuals, influence public policy, and shape the nation's legal and social fabric. Throughout her presidency, Harris was committed to appointing judges who reflected her belief in the importance of fairness, justice, and equality under the law.

MADAM PRESIDENT: THE FIRST TERM OF KAMALA HARRIS

Harris's Judicial Appointments: A Focus on Diversity and Experience

From the beginning of her presidency, Harris made it clear that diversity and experience would be central to her judicial appointments. She believed that the judiciary should reflect the diversity of the American people and that judges should bring a wide range of experiences to the bench, including backgrounds in civil rights, public service, and legal advocacy.

Diversity on the Bench

Harris's commitment to diversity was evident in her nominations to the federal judiciary. She appointed a record number of women, people of color, and individuals from underrepresented communities to the federal courts. This included not only the district and appellate courts but also the Supreme Court, where her appointments had a transformative impact.

Among her notable appointments were:

1. Justice Candace Jackson-Akiwumi: Harris's first appointment to the Supreme Court, Candace Jackson-Akiwumi, was a former public defender and judge on the U.S. Court of Appeals for the Seventh Circuit. Her appointment was historic, making her the first Black woman to serve on the Supreme Court. Jackson-Akiwumi's background in criminal justice reform and her experience as a public defender brought a unique perspective to the Court,

emphasizing the importance of fairness and justice in the legal system.

2. Justice Goodwin Liu: Harris's second appointment to the Supreme Court was Goodwin Liu, a respected legal scholar and judge on the California Supreme Court. Liu, the son of Taiwanese immigrants, was known for his work on constitutional law, civil rights, and education. His appointment further diversified the Court and brought a strong voice for equality and social justice to the bench.

3. Judge Myrna Pérez: Harris also appointed Myrna Pérez, a leading voting rights attorney and advocate, to the U.S. Court of Appeals for the Second Circuit. Pérez's work at the Brennan Center for Justice had focused on protecting voting rights and ensuring fair elections, making her appointment a critical addition to the judiciary at a time when voting rights were under significant threat.

These appointments, along with many others, reflected Harris's commitment to building a judiciary that was not only diverse but also deeply committed to the principles of justice and equality. Her appointees brought a wealth of experience from various fields of law, including civil rights, criminal justice reform, environmental law, and immigration law.

The Impact on the Federal Judiciary

The impact of Harris's appointments on the federal judiciary was profound. By the end of her first term, she had appointed more judges to the federal courts than any president since Franklin D. Roosevelt. Her appointments significantly shifted the ideological balance of the courts, particularly in key appellate circuits that had previously leaned conservative.

Harris's appointments were particularly influential in the Ninth Circuit Court of Appeals, which covers a large portion of the western United States, including California. By appointing progressive judges with backgrounds in civil rights and public interest law, Harris helped to solidify the Ninth Circuit as a bastion of liberal jurisprudence.

The addition of Justice Jackson-Akiwumi and Justice Liu to the Supreme Court also had a lasting impact on the Court's decisions. With these appointments, the Court moved in a more progressive direction on issues such as voting rights, healthcare, and environmental protection. Harris's appointees brought a renewed focus on protecting individual rights, addressing systemic inequalities, and ensuring that the law served the interests of all Americans, not just the powerful.

Key Legal Battles During Harris's Term

While Harris's judicial appointments were critical in shaping the future of American law, her presidency was also defined by a series of key legal battles that tested the limits of executive power, the protection of civil rights, and the role of the judiciary in a polarized society.

Voting Rights and the Fight Against Voter Suppression

One of the most significant legal battles during Harris's presidency was over voting rights. In the wake of the 2020 presidential election, which saw record voter turnout, many states, particularly those with Republican-controlled legislatures, passed new laws aimed at restricting voting access. These laws included measures such as stricter voter ID requirements, reduced early voting, and limitations on mail-in voting, which disproportionately affected communities of color, low-income voters, and young people.

Harris's administration responded by making the protection of voting rights a top priority. The Department of Justice (DOJ), under the leadership of Attorney General Vanita Gupta, filed lawsuits against several states, challenging the constitutionality of these voter suppression laws. The DOJ argued that these laws violated the Voting Rights Act of 1965, the Fourteenth Amendment, and the Fifteenth Amendment, which prohibit racial discrimination in voting and protect the right to vote.

The legal battles over voting rights culminated in a landmark case that reached the Supreme Court: *United States v. Georgia*. In this case, the Harris administration challenged Georgia's new voting law, which included provisions that restricted absentee voting, reduced the number of drop boxes, and made it a crime to provide food or water to voters waiting in line.

In a closely watched decision, the Supreme Court, with Justices Jackson-Akiwumi and Liu playing pivotal roles, ruled in favor of the Harris administration. The Court held that Georgia's law violated the Voting Rights Act and the Constitution by disproportionately burdening minority voters. The decision was hailed as a major victory for voting rights advocates and set a precedent for future challenges to voter suppression laws.

However, the fight over voting rights was far from over. Despite the Supreme Court's ruling, several states continued to pass restrictive voting laws, leading to ongoing legal battles. Harris's administration remained vigilant in its efforts to protect voting rights, and her judicial appointments ensured that the courts would continue to play a critical role in safeguarding this fundamental right.

Healthcare and the Affordable Care Act

Another major legal battle during Harris's presidency centered on healthcare, particularly the future of the Affordable Care Act (ACA). The ACA, also known as "Obamacare," had been a cornerstone of President Barack Obama's legacy and had survived multiple legal challenges over the years. However, after years of attempts to repeal or weaken the law, a new challenge to the ACA emerged during Harris's term.

In Texas v. United States, a coalition of Republican-led states argued that the ACA's individual mandate, which required individuals to purchase health insurance, was unconstitutional after Congress reduced the penalty for not having insurance to zero in 2017. The plaintiffs contended that without the mandate, the entire law should be struck down.

The case made its way to the Supreme Court, where the stakes were high. Striking down the ACA would have had far-reaching consequences, potentially stripping millions of Americans of their health insurance and eliminating protections for those with pre-existing conditions.

Harris's administration vigorously defended the ACA, arguing that the law was constitutional and that its provisions were critical to ensuring access to affordable healthcare for all Americans. The administration also emphasized the importance of the ACA in addressing health disparities, particularly during the ongoing COVID-19 pandemic.

In a 6-3 decision, the Supreme Court upheld the ACA, ruling that the plaintiffs lacked standing to challenge the law. The decision was a major victory for the Harris administration and ensured the continued protection of healthcare coverage for millions of Americans. Justices Jackson-Akiwumi and Liu were instrumental in the decision, with both emphasizing the importance of access to healthcare as a fundamental right.

The ruling also had broader implications for the future of healthcare reform in the United States. With the ACA secure, Harris's administration was able to build on the law's successes by expanding Medicaid, introducing a public option, and pursuing additional reforms to lower healthcare costs and improve access to care.

Executive Power and the Limits of Presidential Authority

Throughout her presidency, Harris faced a number of legal challenges related to the limits of executive power. These challenges often centered on the administration's efforts to address pressing issues such as climate change, immigration, and national security.

One of the most significant legal battles over executive power involved the administration's efforts to combat climate change. Early in her presidency, Harris issued a series of executive orders aimed at reducing greenhouse gas emissions, transitioning the country to renewable energy, and reversing the environmental rollbacks of the previous administration.

However, several of these executive actions were challenged in court by states and industry groups, who argued that the administration had overstepped its authority. In one high-profile case, West Virginia v. Environmental Protection Agency (EPA), a coalition of states and coal industry groups sued the administration over its efforts to regulate carbon emissions from power plants.

The case made its way to the Supreme Court, where the administration argued that the EPA had the authority to regulate greenhouse gas emissions under the Clean Air Act. The plaintiffs, however, contended that the administration's actions represented an unconstitutional expansion of executive power and that such regulations should be left to Congress.

In a closely divided decision, the Supreme Court upheld the administration's authority to regulate greenhouse gas emissions, ruling that the EPA had the power to enforce the Clean Air Act in order to protect public health and the environment. The decision was a significant victory for the Harris administration and affirmed the president's ability to take bold action on climate change through executive orders.

However, the ruling also underscored the ongoing tensions between executive authority and the role of Congress in shaping public policy. While Harris was able to achieve significant progress on climate change through executive action, the legal battles highlighted the limitations of this approach and the importance of building legislative support for lasting reforms.

Long-Term Implications of Harris's Judicial Appointments

As Harris's presidency continued, the long-term implications of her judicial appointments became increasingly clear. The judges and justices she appointed were not only shaping the outcomes of key legal battles during her term, but they were also setting the stage for the future of American law and society.

A Progressive Shift in the Judiciary

MADAM PRESIDENT: THE FIRST TERM OF KAMALA HARRIS

Harris's appointments significantly shifted the ideological balance of the federal judiciary, particularly at the appellate level and the Supreme Court. Her appointees brought a progressive perspective to the bench, emphasizing the protection of individual rights, the advancement of social justice, and the importance of addressing systemic inequalities.

This shift had profound implications for a wide range of legal issues, from civil rights and voting rights to environmental protection and healthcare. Harris's appointees were more likely to rule in favor of protecting the rights of marginalized communities, upholding progressive social policies, and supporting government efforts to address public health and environmental challenges.

The impact of this shift was felt not only in high-profile cases that reached the Supreme Court but also in the thousands of cases decided by lower federal courts each year. Harris's appointees played a key role in shaping the legal landscape on issues such as LGBTQ+ rights, immigration, reproductive rights, and criminal justice reform.

The Legacy of Diversity and Representation

One of the most significant legacies of Harris's judicial appointments was the increased diversity and representation on the federal bench. By appointing a record number of women, people of color, and individuals from underrepresented communities, Harris helped to ensure that the judiciary better reflected the diversity of the American population.

This diversity had important implications for the administration of justice, as judges from different backgrounds brought a wider range of perspectives and experiences to their decision-making. Harris believed that a more diverse judiciary would lead to fairer and more equitable outcomes, particularly in cases involving civil rights and social justice.

The impact of this increased diversity was also felt beyond the courtroom, as Harris's appointments served as a powerful symbol of the progress that had been made in breaking down barriers and expanding opportunities for all Americans. Her appointees became role models for future generations of lawyers and judges, inspiring more young people from diverse backgrounds to pursue careers in the legal profession.

The Enduring Influence of Harris's Appointees

As Harris's first term neared its end, the judges and justices she appointed continued to serve on the federal bench, shaping the interpretation of law for years, and possibly decades, to come. The decisions they rendered would influence the direction of American law and policy on issues ranging from civil liberties and voting rights to environmental protection and healthcare.

The enduring influence of Harris's appointees was particularly evident on the Supreme Court, where Justices

Jackson-Akiwumi and Liu played key roles in shaping the Court's jurisprudence on critical issues. Their decisions, often grounded in a commitment to social justice and equality, would leave a lasting mark on the legal landscape and help to advance the progressive vision that Harris had championed throughout her presidency.

A Lasting Legacy in the Judiciary

Kamala Harris's presidency was marked by significant achievements in a wide range of areas, from healthcare and climate change to economic justice and civil rights. However, one of her most enduring legacies was her impact on the federal judiciary.

Through her judicial appointments, Harris reshaped the federal courts, bringing greater diversity, experience, and a commitment to justice and equality to the bench. Her appointees played a crucial role in key legal battles that defined her presidency, and their decisions would continue to influence American law and society for generations.

Harris's legacy in the judiciary was not only about the decisions her appointees made but also about the broader vision they represented—a vision of a legal system that was fairer, more inclusive, and more responsive to the needs and rights of all Americans. As the nation moved forward, the judges and justices appointed by Harris would serve as guardians of that vision, ensuring that the principles of justice, equality, and the rule of law remained at the heart of the American legal system.

Chapter 18: International Alliances and Global Diplomacy

Rebuilding Trust and Leadership on the Global Stage

When Kamala Harris took office as the 47th President of the United States, the world was at a crossroads. The international order, shaped by decades of U.S. leadership in global institutions, alliances, and diplomacy, was under strain. The rise of new powers, the resurgence of authoritarianism, the intensifying challenges of climate change, and the lingering effects of the COVID-19 pandemic had all contributed to a world in flux. The United States, long seen as a stabilizing force in global affairs, had seen its leadership questioned and its alliances strained.

President Harris understood that to navigate these challenges, the United States needed to reaffirm its commitment to global leadership, rebuild trust with its allies, and forge new partnerships to address the complexities of the 21st century. Her administration embarked on an ambitious agenda to strengthen old alliances, create new ones, and play a leading role in global humanitarian efforts and peacekeeping missions.

Restoring and Strengthening Alliances

A cornerstone of Harris's foreign policy was the restoration and strengthening of traditional alliances that had been the bedrock of U.S. global strategy since the end of World War II. Harris believed that these alliances, particularly with NATO and key partners in Asia, were essential not only for U.S. security but also for global stability and the promotion of democratic values.

Revitalizing NATO

One of Harris's first priorities in office was to revitalize the North Atlantic Treaty Organization (NATO), which had faced challenges in recent years due to internal divisions, questions about burden-sharing, and differing views on how to address emerging threats, such as cyberattacks and terrorism.

Harris worked to rebuild trust and cohesion within the alliance, emphasizing the importance of NATO as a collective defense organization and a pillar of transatlantic security. She reaffirmed the United States' commitment to Article 5 of the NATO Treaty, which states that an attack on one member is an attack on all. This commitment was particularly important in the context of rising tensions with Russia, which had engaged in aggressive actions in Eastern Europe and cyber operations against NATO members.

To demonstrate her commitment to the alliance, Harris increased U.S. contributions to NATO's defense budget and encouraged other member states to do the same. She also supported NATO's efforts to modernize its capabilities, including investments in cyber defense, counterterrorism, and rapid response forces. Harris was a strong advocate for expanding NATO's focus to address new and emerging threats, including climate change and the security implications of technological advancements.

Under Harris's leadership, NATO adopted a new strategic concept that reflected these priorities. The alliance also expanded its partnerships with non-NATO countries, particularly in the Asia-Pacific region, where Harris saw opportunities to counterbalance China's growing influence and assertiveness.

Strengthening Alliances in the Asia-Pacific

In addition to revitalizing NATO, Harris placed a strong emphasis on strengthening U.S. alliances in the Asia-Pacific region. The rise of China as a global power had fundamentally altered the strategic landscape in Asia, and Harris believed that a strong network of alliances was essential for maintaining stability and promoting democratic values in the region.

Key to this effort was the strengthening of the U.S. alliance with Japan, a cornerstone of the U.S. security presence in Asia. Harris worked closely with Japanese Prime Minister Yoshihide Suga to enhance defense cooperation, including the deployment of advanced U.S. military assets in Japan and joint exercises aimed at countering potential threats from North Korea and China. The two leaders also collaborated on economic and technological initiatives, including efforts to secure supply chains and promote innovation in areas such as artificial intelligence and clean energy.

Harris also deepened ties with South Korea, another critical ally in the region. She supported efforts to strengthen the U.S.-South Korea alliance through enhanced military cooperation and intelligence sharing. Harris and South Korean President Moon Jae-in worked together on a range of issues, from addressing the North Korean nuclear threat to promoting regional stability and economic cooperation.

In addition to these traditional alliances, Harris sought to build new partnerships in the Asia-Pacific region. She expanded cooperation with Australia, India, and the Association of Southeast Asian Nations (ASEAN) through the Quadrilateral Security Dialogue, commonly known as the Quad. This informal strategic forum brought together the United States, Japan, India, and Australia to discuss regional security issues and coordinate responses to challenges such as maritime security, counterterrorism, and humanitarian assistance.

The Quad became an increasingly important platform for addressing the strategic challenges posed by China's growing influence in the Indo-Pacific. Harris's administration worked to enhance the Quad's capabilities, including joint military exercises, intelligence sharing, and coordinated diplomatic efforts. The Quad also played a key role in promoting a free and open Indo-Pacific, with a focus on upholding international law, freedom of navigation, and respect for territorial sovereignty.

Forging New Alliances and Partnerships

While strengthening traditional alliances was a central focus of Harris's foreign policy, she also recognized the need to forge new alliances and partnerships to address the complex challenges of the 21st century. These efforts were particularly important in regions where the United States had historically had limited engagement or where new strategic interests had emerged.

The Global Climate Alliance

One of the most significant new alliances forged during Harris's presidency was the Global Climate Alliance, a coalition of countries committed to addressing climate change through ambitious action and international cooperation. Harris recognized that climate change was not only an environmental challenge but also a security threat, with the potential to exacerbate conflicts, displace populations, and disrupt economies.

The Global Climate Alliance brought together countries from every region of the world, including both developed and developing nations, to work towards the goals of the Paris Agreement. Under Harris's leadership, the United States took a leading role in the alliance, committing to substantial reductions in greenhouse gas emissions and providing financial and technical support to help other countries transition to clean energy.

The alliance also focused on building resilience to the impacts of climate change, particularly in vulnerable regions such as the Pacific Islands, Sub-Saharan Africa, and South

Asia. Harris championed initiatives to support climate adaptation, including investments in climate-resilient infrastructure, early warning systems, and sustainable agriculture.

The Global Climate Alliance was not only a diplomatic success but also a demonstration of Harris's commitment to multilateralism and international cooperation. By bringing together countries with diverse interests and capacities, the alliance was able to make significant progress on climate action and set an example for how the international community could come together to address global challenges.

Expanding Engagement in Africa

Harris also sought to expand U.S. engagement in Africa, a continent that she believed was critical to the future of global security, economic growth, and innovation. Her administration recognized that Africa's young and growing population, rich natural resources, and strategic location made it a key region for U.S. foreign policy.

To strengthen U.S.-Africa relations, Harris launched the Africa Partnership Initiative, a comprehensive effort to deepen diplomatic, economic, and security ties with African nations. The initiative focused on four key areas: promoting economic development, supporting democratic governance, enhancing security cooperation, and addressing global challenges such as climate change and public health.

Economic development was a central focus of the initiative, with Harris promoting trade and investment between the United States and African countries. Her administration supported efforts to expand the African Growth and Opportunity Act (AGOA), which provided preferential access to U.S. markets for African exports. Harris also worked to attract U.S. investment in Africa's infrastructure, technology, and energy sectors, recognizing the potential for mutual benefits in these areas.

Harris was also a strong advocate for supporting democratic governance in Africa. She emphasized the importance of free and fair elections, respect for human rights, and the rule of law as the foundation for sustainable development and stability. Her administration provided technical and financial assistance to African countries to strengthen their democratic institutions and support civil society organizations.

Security cooperation was another key component of the Africa Partnership Initiative. Harris worked to enhance partnerships with African nations in areas such as counterterrorism, peacekeeping, and maritime security. The administration provided training and support to African military and law enforcement agencies to help them address security challenges, including the threat posed by extremist groups such as Boko Haram and al-Shabaab.

Finally, the initiative addressed global challenges that disproportionately affected Africa, such as climate change and public health. Harris's administration provided support for climate adaptation and mitigation efforts, as well as assistance in combating infectious diseases such as malaria, HIV/AIDS, and COVID-19.

Latin America and the Caribbean: Renewed Engagement

In Latin America and the Caribbean, Harris sought to renew U.S. engagement in a region that had often been overlooked in recent years. Her administration recognized that the stability and prosperity of the Western Hemisphere were closely linked to U.S. national interests, and she worked to build stronger partnerships with countries in the region.

Harris's approach to Latin America and the Caribbean was rooted in the principles of mutual respect, cooperation, and shared responsibility. She sought to address the root causes of migration from Central America by promoting economic development, improving governance, and enhancing security in the region. The administration launched the Central America Partnership, which provided financial assistance and technical support to help countries in the region address poverty, corruption, and violence.

In addition to addressing migration, Harris worked to strengthen economic ties with Latin America and the Caribbean. Her administration supported efforts to expand trade and investment, particularly in areas such as renewable energy, technology, and infrastructure. Harris also promoted regional integration through initiatives such as the Americas Partnership for Economic Prosperity, which aimed to create a more interconnected and resilient regional economy.

Harris was also committed to supporting democratic governance in Latin America and the Caribbean. Her administration provided assistance to countries in the region to strengthen their democratic institutions, protect human rights, and combat corruption. Harris worked closely with regional organizations such as the Organization of American States (OAS) to promote democracy and the rule of law.

Global Humanitarian Efforts and Peacekeeping Missions

In addition to her focus on alliances and partnerships, Harris's presidency was marked by a strong commitment to global humanitarian efforts and peacekeeping missions. She believed that the United States had a moral responsibility to help those in need and to contribute to global peace and security.

Humanitarian Assistance

One of the most significant global humanitarian efforts undertaken during Harris's presidency was the response to the ongoing refugee crisis in the Middle East and North Africa. The conflict in Syria, along with instability in countries such as Yemen and Libya, had displaced millions of people, creating one of the largest refugee crises in modern history.

Harris's administration took a leading role in the international response to the crisis, providing significant financial assistance to support refugees and host communities. The administration worked closely with international organizations such as the United Nations High Commissioner for Refugees (UNHCR) and the World Food Programme (WFP) to deliver aid, including food, shelter, and healthcare, to those affected by the crisis.

In addition to providing humanitarian assistance, Harris was a strong advocate for resettling refugees in the United States. Her administration increased the number of refugees admitted to the country, reversing the restrictive policies of the previous administration. Harris emphasized that the United States had a long tradition of welcoming those fleeing persecution and that resettling refugees was both a humanitarian imperative and a reflection of American values.

Harris's administration also played a key role in addressing the humanitarian impacts of climate change, particularly in vulnerable regions such as the Pacific Islands, Sub-Saharan Africa, and South Asia. The administration provided support for climate adaptation and resilience efforts, including investments in disaster preparedness, early warning systems, and sustainable development.

Peacekeeping and Conflict Resolution

Harris was a strong supporter of international peacekeeping missions and conflict resolution efforts. She believed that the United States had a responsibility to contribute to global peace and security and that multilateral efforts were essential for addressing conflicts and preventing the spread of violence.

Under Harris's leadership, the United States increased its support for United Nations peacekeeping missions, both financially and through the provision of personnel and resources. Harris recognized the importance of peacekeeping in maintaining stability in conflict-prone regions and preventing the escalation of violence.

One of the most significant peacekeeping efforts during Harris's presidency was the mission in South Sudan. The country had been embroiled in a civil war since its independence in 2011, leading to widespread violence, displacement, and humanitarian suffering. Harris's administration worked closely with the United Nations and regional organizations to support the peace process in South Sudan, including efforts to implement the revitalized peace agreement and promote reconciliation among warring parties.

In addition to supporting peacekeeping missions, Harris played a key role in diplomatic efforts to resolve conflicts through negotiation and dialogue. One of the most notable examples of this was her administration's involvement in the peace talks between Israel and Palestine. Harris worked tirelessly to bring the two sides to the negotiating table, emphasizing the importance of a two-state solution that would ensure security and dignity for both Israelis and Palestinians.

While the peace process in the Middle East remained challenging, Harris's diplomatic efforts were praised for their persistence and commitment to finding a peaceful resolution to one of the world's most intractable conflicts.

Key Diplomatic Successes

Harris's presidency was marked by several key diplomatic successes that demonstrated the effectiveness of her approach to international relations and the evolving role of the United States on the world stage.

Rejoining the Paris Agreement and Leading Global Climate Action

One of the first major diplomatic actions of Harris's presidency was the decision to rejoin the Paris Agreement, which had been a key pillar of global efforts to combat climate change. Harris's commitment to climate action was evident from the outset, and her administration worked to restore U.S. leadership in international climate negotiations.

Harris's leadership on climate change was instrumental in the success of the 2025 United Nations Climate Change Conference (COP30), held in Mexico City. At the conference, the United States played a leading role in negotiating a new global agreement to accelerate climate action, including more ambitious emissions reduction targets, increased financial support for developing countries, and stronger commitments to protect biodiversity and ecosystems.

The success of COP30 was seen as a major diplomatic achievement for Harris, who had made climate change a central focus of her foreign policy. The new agreement, known as the Mexico City Accord, was hailed as a critical step in the global effort to limit global warming to 1.5 degrees Celsius and to build resilience to the impacts of climate change.

The New START Treaty Extension

Another key diplomatic success of Harris's presidency was the extension of the New START Treaty, a critical arms control agreement between the United States and Russia. The treaty, which was set to expire in 2026, limited the number of deployed nuclear warheads and delivery systems on both sides and included rigorous verification measures to ensure compliance.

Harris's administration prioritized the extension of the New START Treaty as a key component of its efforts to reduce the risk of nuclear conflict and to promote global security. Despite challenges in U.S.-Russia relations, Harris and her team were able to negotiate an extension of the treaty for an additional five years, ensuring that the limits on nuclear arsenals would remain in place.

The extension of the New START Treaty was widely regarded as a significant achievement in arms control and a demonstration of Harris's commitment to diplomacy and global security. It also provided a foundation for future negotiations on more comprehensive arms control agreements, including efforts to address new and emerging threats such as cyber warfare and space-based weapons.

MADAM PRESIDENT: THE FIRST TERM OF KAMALA HARRIS

The Abraham Accords Expansion

Building on the diplomatic achievements of the previous administration, Harris's presidency saw the expansion of the Abraham Accords, a series of agreements that normalized relations between Israel and several Arab states, including the United Arab Emirates, Bahrain, and Morocco.

Harris's administration worked to build on the momentum of the Abraham Accords by encouraging additional countries in the Middle East and North Africa to establish diplomatic relations with Israel. These efforts were successful, with several more countries, including Oman and Sudan, joining the accords.

The expansion of the Abraham Accords was seen as a significant diplomatic success, contributing to greater stability and cooperation in the Middle East. Harris emphasized the importance of these agreements not only for regional security but also for promoting economic development, cultural exchange, and people-to-people ties between Israel and its Arab neighbors.

The Evolving Role of the U.S. on the World Stage

As Harris's presidency progressed, it became clear that her approach to international alliances and global diplomacy was shaping the evolving role of the United States on the world stage. Harris's leadership emphasized multilateralism, cooperation, and the importance of addressing global challenges through collective action.

A Recommitment to Multilateralism

One of the defining features of Harris's foreign policy was her recommitment to multilateralism and international institutions. Harris believed that the United States could not address the complex challenges of the 21st century—such as climate change, pandemics, and global inequality—on its own. Instead, she argued that effective solutions required collaboration with other countries and a strong commitment to the rules-based international order.

Harris's administration worked to strengthen the United Nations, the World Health Organization (WHO), and other international organizations, providing financial support, technical expertise, and leadership in key initiatives. Harris also sought to reform these institutions to make them more effective, accountable, and responsive to the needs of the global community.

Promoting Global Health and Pandemic Preparedness

The COVID-19 pandemic had underscored the importance of global health and pandemic preparedness, and Harris made these issues a central focus of her foreign policy. Her administration played a leading role in global efforts to combat the pandemic, including the distribution of vaccines, the strengthening of health systems, and the support for research and development of new treatments and technologies.

Harris's administration also worked to strengthen international cooperation on pandemic preparedness, including efforts to establish a global health security framework that would improve early warning systems, enhance surveillance and response capabilities, and ensure equitable access to medical countermeasures.

Advancing Human Rights and Democratic Values

Throughout her presidency, Harris was a strong advocate for advancing human rights and democratic values on the world stage. Her administration supported efforts to protect freedom of expression, promote gender equality, and combat discrimination and violence against marginalized communities.

Harris was also a vocal critic of authoritarianism and human rights abuses, using diplomacy and economic tools such as sanctions to hold governments accountable for their actions. She worked closely with allies to support pro-democracy movements and to strengthen democratic institutions in countries facing political instability and repression.

A Legacy of Global Leadership

As Kamala Harris's presidency drew to a close, her approach to international alliances and global diplomacy left a lasting impact on the world stage. Harris's efforts to strengthen old alliances, forge new partnerships, and lead global humanitarian efforts demonstrated the United States' renewed commitment to multilateralism, cooperation, and the promotion of democratic values.

Her administration's diplomatic successes, from the expansion of the Abraham Accords to the negotiation of the Mexico City Accord on climate change, were seen as significant achievements that advanced global security, prosperity, and sustainability.

Harris's legacy in global diplomacy was one of leadership and vision, grounded in the belief that the United States could and should play a leading role in addressing the world's most pressing challenges. Her presidency reaffirmed the importance of alliances, partnerships, and international institutions in shaping a more peaceful, just, and resilient world. As the United States continued to navigate the complexities of the 21st century, the foundations laid by Harris's foreign policy would serve as a guide for future leaders in their pursuit of global peace and progress.

Chapter 19: The Road to Re-Election

The Final Year: Preparing for the Next Chapter

As Kamala Harris approached the final year of her first term as the 47th President of the United States, the atmosphere in Washington and across the country was charged with anticipation. The achievements and challenges of the past three years had shaped the political landscape and set the stage for what was expected to be a fiercely contested re-election campaign. For Harris, the road to re-election was not just about securing another term in office; it was about defending her administration's record, building on its successes, and laying out a vision for the future that resonated with the American people.

Throughout her first term, Harris had faced numerous trials, from navigating a global economic downturn to managing domestic crises and addressing deep-seated issues of inequality, justice, and climate change. As the country prepared for the 2028 presidential election, the focus was on how Harris's leadership had shaped the nation and what her re-election bid would mean for the future.

Reflecting on the Administration's Achievements

As Harris's administration prepared for the upcoming election, it was essential to reflect on the significant achievements of her first term. These accomplishments would form the cornerstone of her re-election campaign, serving as a testament to her leadership and the progress made under her administration.

Economic Recovery and Growth

One of the most notable achievements of Harris's presidency was her administration's successful navigation of the global economic downturn of 2027. Faced with a severe economic crisis that threatened to surpass the Great Recession, Harris had taken decisive action to stabilize financial markets, support workers and businesses, and lay the groundwork for a robust recovery.

The implementation of the Economic Security and Recovery Act, the American Renewal Initiative, and other key measures had helped to restore confidence in the economy, create jobs, and promote sustainable growth. By the end of 2027, the U.S. economy was on a strong trajectory, with unemployment at historic lows, wage growth outpacing inflation, and new industries emerging as drivers of innovation and prosperity.

Harris's economic policies had also been successful in addressing long-standing issues of inequality and economic insecurity. The Fair Share Tax Act, the Raise the Wage Act, and the expansion of social welfare programs had helped to reduce the wealth gap, improve living standards for working families, and provide a stronger safety net for those in need.

As Harris looked ahead to the 2028 election, she could point to the administration's economic achievements as evidence of her ability to lead the country through crisis and deliver results that benefited all Americans.

Healthcare Reform and Access

Another key theme of Harris's first term was her administration's commitment to expanding access to healthcare and building on the successes of the Affordable Care Act (ACA). Harris had made healthcare reform a central focus of her presidency, and her administration had delivered on this promise with significant legislative victories.

The introduction of a public option, the expansion of Medicaid, and the reforms to reduce prescription drug prices had all contributed to a more accessible and affordable healthcare system. The Harris administration's defense of the ACA in the Supreme Court, culminating in the landmark decision to uphold the law, had also ensured that millions of Americans would continue to have access to healthcare coverage.

These healthcare achievements were particularly significant in the context of the ongoing public health challenges, including the long-term impacts of the COVID-19 pandemic and the administration's efforts to strengthen public health infrastructure and pandemic preparedness.

As the 2028 election approached, Harris's record on healthcare would be a central theme of her re-election campaign, highlighting her commitment to ensuring that all Americans had access to quality, affordable care.

Climate Leadership and Environmental Justice

Climate change had been a defining issue of Harris's presidency, and her administration had made significant strides in advancing climate action and environmental justice. From rejoining the Paris Agreement to leading the negotiation of the Mexico City Accord, Harris had positioned the United States as a global leader in the fight against climate change.

Domestically, the administration's efforts to transition to clean energy, reduce greenhouse gas emissions, and invest in climate resilience had set the country on a path toward a more sustainable future. The Green New Deal initiatives, combined with investments in renewable energy, electric vehicles, and energy efficiency, had created jobs, spurred innovation, and reduced the nation's reliance on fossil fuels.

Harris's commitment to environmental justice had also been a key focus of her administration, with policies aimed at addressing the disproportionate impacts of climate change and environmental degradation on marginalized communities. The establishment of the Environmental Justice Task Force and the implementation of targeted programs to support vulnerable populations had helped to ensure that the benefits of climate action were shared equitably.

MADAM PRESIDENT: THE FIRST TERM OF KAMALA HARRIS

As Harris prepared for the 2028 election, her record on climate change and environmental justice would be a major selling point, particularly for younger voters and those concerned about the future of the planet.

Justice and Equality

Throughout her first term, Harris had been a champion of justice and equality, working to address systemic inequalities and protect the rights of all Americans. Her administration's efforts to reform the criminal justice system, protect voting rights, and advance civil rights had been central to this mission.

The administration's judicial appointments, including the historic appointments of Justice Candace Jackson-Akiwumi and Justice Goodwin Liu to the Supreme Court, had helped to shape a more progressive and diverse judiciary. These appointments, along with the administration's defense of key civil rights legislation, had ensured that the courts would continue to play a vital role in protecting the rights of marginalized communities.

Harris's efforts to combat voter suppression, strengthen voting rights, and ensure fair elections had also been a significant focus of her presidency. The administration's victories in key legal battles, such as United States v. Georgia, had reaffirmed the importance of protecting the right to vote and ensuring that all Americans had a voice in the democratic process.

As Harris looked ahead to the 2028 election, her record on justice and equality would be a central theme, resonating with voters who were committed to building a more just and inclusive society.

Global Leadership and Diplomacy

On the international stage, Harris's presidency had been marked by a renewed commitment to global leadership, multilateralism, and diplomacy. Her administration had worked to strengthen traditional alliances, forge new partnerships, and address global challenges through collective action.

Key diplomatic successes, such as the expansion of the Abraham Accords, the extension of the New START Treaty, and the leadership role in the Global Climate Alliance, had demonstrated Harris's ability to navigate complex international issues and advance U.S. interests on the world stage.

Harris's commitment to global humanitarian efforts, peacekeeping missions, and the promotion of human rights and democratic values had further solidified her reputation as a leader who was committed to upholding the principles of justice and cooperation in international affairs.

As the 2028 election approached, Harris's record on global leadership would be a key component of her re-election campaign, appealing to voters who valued a strong and engaged U.S. presence in the world.

Challenges and Criticisms: Navigating a Polarized Landscape

While Harris's administration had achieved significant successes, her first term had not been without its challenges and criticisms. The political landscape remained deeply polarized, and the road to re-election would require navigating a complex and often contentious environment.

Economic Concerns

Despite the administration's success in managing the economic downturn and promoting recovery, concerns about inflation, income inequality, and the cost of living continued to weigh on the minds of many voters. Some critics argued that the administration's policies, particularly the expansion of social welfare programs and increased government spending, had contributed to rising prices and economic uncertainty.

Harris's re-election campaign would need to address these concerns head-on, emphasizing the administration's efforts to create jobs, support working families, and ensure that the benefits of economic growth were shared equitably.

Healthcare Challenges

While the administration had made significant strides in expanding access to healthcare, challenges remained in addressing the rising costs of care and ensuring that all Americans had access to the services they needed. Critics of the administration's healthcare policies argued that the public option and other reforms had not gone far enough in controlling costs and improving access, particularly in rural and underserved areas.

Harris's re-election campaign would need to articulate a clear vision for the future of healthcare, building on the successes of her first term while addressing the remaining gaps and challenges in the system.

Climate and Energy

Harris's ambitious climate agenda had been praised by many, but it had also faced pushback from certain sectors of the economy, particularly the fossil fuel industry and regions heavily dependent on traditional energy sources. Critics argued that the administration's policies had led to job losses in these sectors and had not provided sufficient support for workers transitioning to new industries.

Harris's re-election campaign would need to emphasize the administration's efforts to create new jobs in the clean energy sector, support workers in the transition, and promote a just and equitable energy transition.

Foreign Policy and National Security

While Harris had been successful in strengthening alliances and promoting global cooperation, her foreign policy had not been without its challenges. Tensions with China, Russia, and other global powers had persisted, and the administration had faced criticism for its handling of certain international crises.

MADAM PRESIDENT: THE FIRST TERM OF KAMALA HARRIS

Harris's re-election campaign would need to highlight her administration's achievements in global diplomacy while addressing concerns about national security and the evolving global landscape.

The Political Strategy: Building a Coalition for Re-Election

As Harris's administration prepared for the 2028 election, the focus shifted to building a political strategy that could secure a second term in office. This strategy would need to be multifaceted, addressing the concerns of different voter demographics, energizing the Democratic base, and appealing to swing voters in key battleground states.

Mobilizing the Democratic Base

One of the key components of Harris's re-election strategy was mobilizing the Democratic base, particularly those who had been instrumental in her first election victory. This included women, people of color, young voters, and progressives who were committed to issues such as healthcare, climate change, and social justice.

Harris's campaign would need to build on the enthusiasm of these voters by highlighting her administration's achievements in these areas and outlining a bold vision for the future. This included continuing to champion issues such as reproductive rights, LGBTQ+ rights, and racial justice, which were central to the Democratic base.

Appealing to Swing Voters

In addition to mobilizing the base, Harris's re-election campaign would need to appeal to swing voters, particularly in key battleground states that would determine the outcome of the election. This included moderate and independent voters who were concerned about issues such as the economy, national security, and government accountability.

Harris's campaign would need to emphasize her record of leadership and competence, particularly in managing the economy, addressing public health challenges, and navigating complex international issues. The campaign would also need to articulate a clear and pragmatic vision for the future, addressing the concerns of these voters while maintaining the support of the Democratic base.

Addressing Regional Concerns

Harris's re-election strategy also included efforts to address regional concerns and build support in areas that had been less favorable to her administration. This included outreach to rural communities, industrial regions, and areas affected by the transition to clean energy.

The campaign would need to emphasize the administration's efforts to support economic development in these regions, including investments in infrastructure, job training, and support for small businesses. Harris would also need to articulate a clear vision for how her administration would continue to support these communities in the future, ensuring that they were not left behind in the nation's transition to a more sustainable and equitable economy.

The Emerging Contenders: A Divided Opposition

As Harris prepared for her re-election campaign, the political landscape on the Republican side was marked by division and uncertainty. The Republican Party, which had struggled to find a unifying message in the wake of the 2024 election, was facing an internal struggle between its establishment wing and a more populist, nationalist faction.

Several potential contenders for the Republican nomination had emerged, each representing different wings of the party and different visions for the country's future.

The Establishment Candidates

On one side of the Republican Party were the establishment candidates, who represented the more traditional, pro-business wing of the party. These candidates emphasized fiscal conservatism, free-market principles, and a strong national defense. They were critical of Harris's economic policies, particularly her expansion of social welfare programs and her approach to regulation and taxation.

Among the leading establishment candidates were Senator Mitt Romney, who had previously run for president in 2012, and Governor Nikki Haley, who had served as U.S. Ambassador to the United Nations under a previous administration. Both Romney and Haley were seen as experienced and pragmatic leaders who could appeal to moderate voters and build a broad coalition within the party.

The Populist Candidates

On the other side of the Republican Party were the populist candidates, who represented a more nationalist, anti-establishment wing of the party. These candidates emphasized issues such as immigration, trade, and cultural identity, and they were critical of the Republican establishment for failing to address the concerns of working-class voters.

Among the leading populist candidates were Senator Josh Hawley, known for his vocal opposition to big tech and globalism, and Governor Ron DeSantis, who had gained national attention for his handling of the COVID-19 pandemic in Florida. Both Hawley and DeSantis were seen as potential heirs to the populist movement that had reshaped the Republican Party in recent years.

The Uncertainty of the Republican Primary

The Republican primary was shaping up to be a contentious and unpredictable race, with no clear frontrunner and deep divisions within the party. The outcome of the primary would have significant implications for the general election, particularly in terms of the direction the Republican Party would take and the message it would present to voters.

For Harris and her campaign, the uncertainty of the Republican primary presented both opportunities and challenges. On the one hand, a divided opposition could make it easier for Harris to build a broad coalition of voters and secure a second term. On the other hand, the emergence of a strong populist candidate could energize the Republican base and create a more competitive general election.

The Road Ahead: A Vision for the Future

As Harris prepared for the 2028 election, she and her campaign team were focused on articulating a clear and compelling vision for the future. This vision would need to build on the successes of her first term while addressing the challenges that remained and outlining a path forward for the country.

A Just and Equitable Economy

Harris's vision for the future included a commitment to building a more just and equitable economy, where all Americans had the opportunity to succeed. This included continuing to support working families through policies such as paid family leave, affordable childcare, and expanded access to education and job training.

Harris also emphasized the importance of addressing economic inequality, particularly through tax reform, wage increases, and support for small businesses and entrepreneurs. Her administration would continue to focus on creating good-paying jobs, particularly in emerging industries such as clean energy and technology, and ensuring that the benefits of economic growth were shared equitably.

Universal Healthcare and Public Health

Another key component of Harris's vision was the continued expansion of access to healthcare and the strengthening of public health infrastructure. Harris's administration would work to build on the successes of the ACA by expanding the public option, reducing prescription drug prices, and ensuring that all Americans had access to affordable, quality care.

Harris also emphasized the importance of preparing for future public health challenges, including pandemics, by investing in research, strengthening the nation's health systems, and ensuring equitable access to vaccines and treatments.

Climate Action and Environmental Justice

Climate action would remain a central focus of Harris's second term, with continued efforts to reduce greenhouse gas emissions, transition to clean energy, and build resilience to the impacts of climate change. Harris's administration would also continue to prioritize environmental justice, ensuring that the benefits of climate action were shared equitably and that vulnerable communities were protected from the impacts of environmental degradation.

Global Leadership and Diplomacy

On the international stage, Harris's vision included a continued commitment to global leadership, multilateralism, and the promotion of democratic values.

Her administration would work to strengthen alliances, forge new partnerships, and address global challenges through collective action.

Harris also emphasized the importance of promoting human rights and democratic governance around the world, using diplomacy, economic tools, and international cooperation to hold governments accountable and support pro-democracy movements.

A More Just and Inclusive Society

Finally, Harris's vision for the future included a commitment to building a more just and inclusive society, where all Americans had the opportunity to thrive. This included continuing to address systemic inequalities, protect civil rights, and ensure that the nation's institutions were fair, accountable, and responsive to the needs of all citizens.

Harris's administration would work to strengthen voting rights, reform the criminal justice system, and promote policies that advanced gender equality, racial justice, and LGBTQ+ rights.

The Journey Continues

As Kamala Harris prepared for the 2028 election, she reflected on the journey that had brought her to this point—the challenges she had faced, the progress she had made, and the vision she had for the future. The road to re-election would not be easy, but Harris was confident in her ability to lead the country through the next chapter and to build a brighter, more just, and more prosperous future for all Americans.

The themes of her first term—economic recovery, healthcare reform, climate action, justice, and global leadership—would continue to guide her as she sought a second term in office. Harris's campaign would be about more than just securing another four years in the White House; it would be about continuing the work she had started and ensuring that the United States remained a beacon of hope, opportunity, and justice in the world.

As the 2028 election approached, the nation watched closely, ready to decide whether to continue the journey with Kamala Harris or to chart a new course. For Harris, the road to re-election was about more than just politics; it was about the future of the country and the legacy she hoped to leave for generations to come.

Chapter 20: Legacy and Reflection

Securing a Second Term: The 2028 Election

Kamala Harris's re-election in 2028 was a defining moment in American political history, not just for her own legacy but for the broader trajectory of the United States. Her victory was decisive, with Harris securing a large number of electoral votes and winning the popular vote by a comfortable margin. The election, which saw her running against the Republican candidate, Governor Ron DeSantis of Florida, was closely watched both at home and abroad. DeSantis, a prominent figure in the populist wing of the Republican Party, had campaigned on a platform that emphasized nationalism, immigration restrictions, and a rollback of many of Harris's policies.

Despite a contentious and polarizing campaign, Harris's message of progress, unity, and a vision for a sustainable and equitable future resonated with a broad coalition of voters. Her running mate, Alexandria Ocasio-Cortez, a dynamic and influential congresswoman from New York, brought energy and a progressive vision that appealed particularly to younger voters, women, and communities of color. Together, Harris and Ocasio-Cortez presented a formidable ticket that combined experience with a bold vision for the future, capturing the imagination of the electorate.

Harris's second term was not just a continuation of her first; it was an opportunity to cement her legacy and to address the challenges and opportunities that had emerged during her first four years in office. As the first female president and the first person of Black and South Asian descent to hold the office, Harris's re-election was also a powerful affirmation of the progress the nation had made toward inclusion and representation in its highest office.

A Legacy of Firsts: Breaking Barriers and Shaping History

Kamala Harris's presidency was marked by a series of historic firsts that would forever be etched in the annals of American history. Her election as the first female president of the United States was a watershed moment, shattering a glass ceiling that had long seemed impenetrable. For millions of women and girls across the country and around the world, Harris's rise to the highest office in the land was a source of inspiration and a powerful reminder that no barrier was insurmountable.

Harris's presidency also carried significant symbolic weight as the first woman of color to lead the nation. Her background as the daughter of immigrants—a Jamaican father and an Indian mother—brought a diverse and multifaceted perspective to the White House. Harris's story resonated with many Americans, particularly those from immigrant and minority communities who saw in her a reflection of their own struggles, aspirations, and achievements.

MADAM PRESIDENT: THE FIRST TERM OF KAMALA HARRIS

Throughout her presidency, Harris was acutely aware of the significance of her role as a trailblazer. She often spoke about the responsibility she felt to open doors for those who would come after her, to ensure that her presidency was not an anomaly but the beginning of a new era of leadership that reflected the true diversity of the American people. Harris's emphasis on representation extended beyond her own identity; it was a central theme in her administration's policies, judicial appointments, and efforts to promote equity and inclusion across all sectors of society.

The Long-Term Effects of Her Policies

Harris's presidency was characterized by an ambitious policy agenda that sought to address some of the most pressing issues facing the United States and the world. Her administration's efforts to promote economic recovery, expand access to healthcare, combat climate change, and advance social justice were central to her legacy. As her second term began, the long-term effects of these policies were becoming increasingly evident.

Economic Resilience and Inclusivity

One of Harris's most significant achievements was her administration's successful navigation of the global economic downturn and the subsequent recovery. The policies implemented during her first term, including the Economic Security and Recovery Act and the American Renewal Initiative, had helped to stabilize the economy, create jobs, and promote sustainable growth. As a result, the

United States entered Harris's second term with a strong and resilient economy.

The administration's focus on economic inclusivity had also made a lasting impact. By raising the minimum wage, expanding access to affordable childcare, and implementing tax reforms that ensured the wealthiest Americans paid their fair share, Harris had helped to reduce income inequality and lift millions of Americans out of poverty. These policies had not only improved the economic well-being of individuals and families but had also contributed to a more stable and equitable economy.

The investments in infrastructure, clean energy, and technology made during Harris's first term had also positioned the United States as a leader in the industries of the future. The creation of green jobs, the expansion of broadband access to rural and underserved communities, and the development of advanced manufacturing capabilities had all contributed to a more dynamic and competitive economy.

As the world faced ongoing challenges, including technological disruption and the transition to a low-carbon economy, Harris's policies were seen as having laid the groundwork for continued economic resilience and innovation.

Healthcare for All

Harris's commitment to expanding access to healthcare was another cornerstone of her legacy. Her administration's efforts to build on the successes of the Affordable Care Act, introduce a public option, and reduce prescription drug prices had transformed the U.S. healthcare system. By the time she entered her second term, millions more Americans had access to affordable healthcare, and the nation was better prepared to address public health challenges.

The administration's focus on public health infrastructure and pandemic preparedness had also made a lasting impact. The investments in research, early warning systems, and healthcare delivery had strengthened the nation's ability to respond to future public health crises, ensuring that the lessons learned from the COVID-19 pandemic were not forgotten.

Harris's healthcare policies had also emphasized equity, with targeted efforts to reduce health disparities and ensure that all Americans, regardless of their income, race, or geographic location, had access to the care they needed. These efforts had helped to address the deep-seated inequalities that had long plagued the U.S. healthcare system, contributing to better health outcomes for underserved communities.

Climate Leadership

Harris's presidency had been defined by her unwavering commitment to climate action, and the long-term effects of her policies were beginning to take shape. Her administration's efforts to reduce greenhouse gas emissions, transition to renewable energy, and build climate resilience had positioned the United States as a global leader in the fight against climate change.

The implementation of the Green New Deal initiatives, combined with the U.S. leadership role in the Global Climate Alliance, had contributed to significant progress in reducing carbon emissions and promoting sustainable development. The investments in clean energy, electric vehicles, and energy efficiency had not only created jobs but had also reduced the nation's reliance on fossil fuels, making the U.S. economy more resilient to energy price shocks.

Harris's emphasis on environmental justice had also made a lasting impact. By addressing the disproportionate impacts of climate change and environmental degradation on marginalized communities, her administration had ensured that the benefits of climate action were shared equitably. The establishment of the Environmental Justice Task Force and the implementation of targeted programs to support vulnerable populations had set a new standard for how climate policy could be both effective and just.

As the world continued to grapple with the realities of climate change, Harris's legacy as a climate leader would be remembered for her bold and decisive action, as well as her commitment to ensuring that no one was left behind in the transition to a sustainable future.

Justice and Civil Rights

Harris's presidency had been marked by a strong commitment to justice and civil rights, and her administration's efforts in these areas had left a lasting legacy. The reforms to the criminal justice system, the protection of voting rights, and the advancement of civil rights had all contributed to a more just and inclusive society.

The administration's judicial appointments, including the historic appointments of Justices Candace Jackson-Akiwumi and Goodwin Liu, had helped to shape a more progressive and diverse judiciary. These judges and justices, along with those appointed to lower federal courts, had played a critical role in protecting civil rights, addressing systemic inequalities, and upholding the principles of justice and equality.

Harris's efforts to combat voter suppression, strengthen voting rights, and ensure fair elections had also made a lasting impact on American democracy. The administration's victories in key legal battles, such as *United States v. Georgia*, had reaffirmed the importance of protecting the right to vote and ensuring that all Americans had a voice in the democratic process.

As Harris's second term began, the long-term effects of her justice and civil rights policies were becoming increasingly evident. The progress made during her first term had set the stage for continued efforts to address systemic inequalities and build a more just and inclusive society.

Global Leadership

On the international stage, Harris's presidency had been marked by a renewed commitment to global leadership, multilateralism, and the promotion of democratic values. Her administration's efforts to strengthen traditional alliances, forge new partnerships, and address global challenges through collective action had solidified the United States' role as a leader in the world.

The success of the Global Climate Alliance, the extension of the New START Treaty, and the expansion of the Abraham Accords were all examples of Harris's effective diplomacy and her ability to navigate complex international issues. Her administration's commitment to global humanitarian efforts, peacekeeping missions, and the promotion of human rights had further demonstrated the United States' role as a force for good in the world.

As Harris's second term began, the long-term effects of her global leadership were becoming increasingly evident. The United States was seen as a reliable and engaged partner in addressing global challenges, and Harris's legacy as a leader who prioritized cooperation, diplomacy, and justice was firmly established.

A Leadership Style Rooted in Empathy and Pragmatism

One of the defining characteristics of Harris's leadership style was her ability to combine empathy with pragmatism. Throughout her presidency, Harris had demonstrated a deep understanding of the challenges facing ordinary Americans, and she had worked tirelessly to address those challenges in a practical and effective manner.

Harris's background as a prosecutor and her experience as a U.S. Senator had given her a unique perspective on the importance of justice, fairness, and accountability. She had brought this perspective to the White House, where she emphasized the importance of listening to diverse voices, building consensus, and finding common ground.

At the same time, Harris was known for her pragmatic approach to governance. She understood the complexities of policy-making and was committed to finding solutions that worked in the real world. This pragmatism was evident in her administration's approach to issues such as economic recovery, healthcare reform, and climate action, where Harris had sought to balance bold action with practical considerations.

Harris's leadership style was also characterized by her ability to inspire and motivate those around her. Whether it was through her speeches, her interactions with everyday Americans, or her work with international leaders, Harris had a unique ability to connect with people and to convey a sense of hope and possibility.

As her second term began, Harris's leadership style continued to shape her approach to governance. Her ability to combine empathy with pragmatism, to listen to diverse voices, and to build consensus would remain central to her efforts to address the challenges and opportunities of the future.

Setting the Stage for the Future

Before she began her second term, her presidency had already set the stage for the future of American politics. Her leadership had demonstrated that it was possible to govern with empathy, pragmatism, and a commitment to justice and equality, even in the face of significant challenges.

The partnership between Harris and Tim Walz, and later, Alexandria Ocasio-Cortez had also highlighted the importance of intergenerational leadership and the power of collaboration between experienced leaders and rising stars. Ocasio-Cortez, who had become a prominent figure in her own right, was widely seen as a potential future presidential candidate, and her work with Harris had positioned her as a key leader in the Democratic Party.

The broader impact of Harris's presidency on American society was also clear. Her administration's efforts to promote diversity, inclusion, and equity had helped to reshape the nation's institutions and to create a more just and inclusive society. The policies and initiatives she had championed would continue to influence American life for years to come, shaping the future of the country in ways that would be felt by generations.

A Legacy of Leadership and Progress

As Kamala Harris entered her second term as President of the United States, her legacy was already taking shape. Her presidency had been marked by historic achievements, from breaking barriers as the first female president to leading the nation through a time of significant challenges and change.

MADAM PRESIDENT: THE FIRST TERM OF KAMALA HARRIS

Harris's leadership had left a lasting impact on the United States and the world, with policies that promoted economic resilience, healthcare access, climate action, and social justice. Her commitment to global leadership, multilateralism, and the promotion of democratic values had strengthened the United States' role on the world stage and demonstrated the power of diplomacy and cooperation.

As she looked ahead to the future, Harris's legacy would be defined not only by her achievements but also by the values and principles that had guided her leadership. Her presidency had shown that it was possible to lead with empathy, to govern with pragmatism, and to inspire with a vision for a better future.

Harris' impact on American society and the world would endure. She had set a new standard for leadership in the 21st century, one that emphasized inclusion, justice, and the importance of working together to address the challenges of our time. As the nation looked to the future, the legacy of Kamala Harris would continue to shape the path forward, offering a vision of a more just, equitable, and prosperous world for all.

Inauguration Address of President Kamala Harris: January 20, 2025

MY FELLOW AMERICANS,

Standing before you today, I am profoundly humbled and deeply honored to be sworn in as the 47th President of the United States of America. This moment is a testament to the resilience, strength, and enduring spirit of our democracy. It is a reflection of the progress we have made as a nation and the challenges we have overcome together. It is also a moment of profound responsibility, one that I do not take lightly.

Today, I stand on the shoulders of those who came before me—leaders, activists, dreamers, and everyday Americans who have fought for justice, equality, and the promise of a better tomorrow. I stand here as the first woman, the first Black woman, and the first person of South Asian descent to hold this office, and I am mindful of what this means for our nation. This is a moment that belongs to all of us, to every American who has believed in the power of our democracy and the possibility of progress.

But as we gather here on this historic day, we do so at a time of great challenge. Our nation faces deep divisions, economic uncertainty, and a rapidly changing world. We have been tested by a global pandemic, an economic downturn, and threats to our democracy. Yet, even in the face of these challenges, I am filled with hope. Hope for our future, hope for our country, and hope for the enduring strength of the American people.

Today, as I take the oath of office, I pledge to you that I will work tirelessly to serve all Americans, to listen to your voices, and to lead with compassion, integrity, and a commitment to justice. Together, we will face the challenges ahead and build a future that reflects the values we hold dear.

Our first task, and perhaps our most important task, is to unite our country. We must bridge the divides that have fractured our nation and heal the wounds that have been inflicted by years of polarization and division. This will not be easy, and it will not happen overnight, but it is essential for the future of our democracy.

I believe that we are stronger when we come together, when we find common ground and work toward a shared vision of a better future. Our diversity is our strength, and it is our duty to ensure that every American, regardless of race, religion, gender, or background, has a seat at the table. We must reject the forces of hatred, intolerance, and division, and instead embrace the values of inclusion, respect, and empathy.

In the coming days, weeks, and months, I will work with leaders from both parties, from all regions of our country, to find solutions to the challenges we face. I will listen to your concerns, seek out your ideas, and work to build consensus. I know that we will not always agree, but I believe that we can find common ground and work together for the good of our nation.

To those who did not vote for me, I want you to know that I will be your president too. I will work to earn your trust, to understand your concerns, and to represent your interests. My door will always be open, and I will always be willing to listen.

To those who feel left behind or forgotten, I want you to know that you are not alone. Your voices matter, your experiences matter, and your future matters. I will work to ensure that our government is responsive to your needs, that our economy works for everyone, and that our society is one where every person has the opportunity to succeed.

Our economy is at a crossroads. The global economic downturn, exacerbated by the COVID-19 pandemic, has left millions of Americans struggling to make ends meet. Families have lost their jobs, businesses have closed their doors, and communities have been devastated. The economic inequality that existed before the pandemic has only deepened, leaving many of our fellow citizens behind.

But I believe in the resilience of the American people and the strength of our economy. We have faced challenges before, and we have always emerged stronger. Now is the time to rebuild our economy in a way that is fair, just, and inclusive. We must create an economy that works for everyone, not just the wealthy and powerful.

To achieve this, we will implement a bold economic recovery plan that focuses on creating good-paying jobs, supporting small businesses, and investing in the industries of the future. We will prioritize infrastructure projects that modernize our transportation networks, expand broadband access, and build the clean energy economy of tomorrow. These investments will not only create jobs, but they will also lay the foundation for long-term economic growth.

We will also address the root causes of economic inequality by raising the minimum wage, expanding access to affordable childcare, and ensuring that every American has access to quality healthcare. We will reform our tax code to ensure that the wealthiest Americans and corporations pay their fair share, and we will close the loopholes that have allowed them to avoid paying what they owe.

But economic recovery is not just about numbers on a balance sheet. It is about people. It is about ensuring that every American has the opportunity to succeed, to provide for their family, and to build a better future. We will work to create an economy that is fair, just, and inclusive—an economy that works for everyone.

The COVID-19 pandemic has shown us the critical importance of a strong and accessible healthcare system. Too many Americans have faced the unimaginable—losing a loved one, struggling with long-term health effects, or facing financial ruin due to medical bills. This is unacceptable, and it is a reminder that healthcare is not a privilege; it is a right.

As your president, I am committed to expanding access to healthcare for all Americans. We will build on the successes of the Affordable Care Act by introducing a public option that provides an affordable alternative to private insurance. This will ensure that every American has access to quality, affordable healthcare, regardless of their income or employment status.

We will also work to reduce the cost of prescription drugs, which have become unaffordable for too many families. We will allow Medicare to negotiate drug prices, cap out-of-pocket costs for seniors, and hold pharmaceutical companies accountable for price gouging.

But expanding access to healthcare is about more than just addressing immediate needs. It is about building a healthcare system that is equitable, sustainable, and responsive to the needs of all Americans. We will work to reduce health disparities by addressing the social determinants of health, such as housing, education, and access to nutritious food. We will invest in preventive care, mental health services, and addiction treatment to ensure that every American has the support they need to live a healthy and fulfilling life.

And we will strengthen our public health infrastructure to ensure that we are prepared for future pandemics and public health emergencies. We have learned hard lessons from the COVID-19 pandemic, and we must ensure that we are never caught unprepared again.

MADAM PRESIDENT: THE FIRST TERM OF KAMALA HARRIS

Climate change is the existential threat of our time, and it is a challenge that we must confront with urgency and resolve. The science is clear: We must take bold action now to reduce greenhouse gas emissions, transition to clean energy, and protect our planet for future generations.

As your president, I am committed to making the United States a global leader in the fight against climate change. We will rejoin the Paris Agreement and work with our international partners to achieve the goals of the agreement. But we will not stop there. We will go further, setting ambitious targets for reducing emissions and investing in the clean energy technologies that will power our future.

We will implement a Green New Deal that creates millions of good-paying jobs in the clean energy sector, from building solar panels and wind turbines to retrofitting buildings and electrifying our transportation system. These jobs will not only help us reduce our carbon footprint, but they will also provide economic opportunities for communities that have been left behind.

We will also invest in climate resilience, ensuring that our communities are prepared for the impacts of climate change, from rising sea levels to more frequent and severe storms. We will prioritize environmental justice, addressing the disproportionate impact of climate change and pollution on low-income communities and communities of color.

But tackling climate change is not just about protecting our planet; it is about building a more just and equitable society.

It is about ensuring that every person has access to clean air, clean water, and a healthy environment. It is about leaving a legacy for our children and grandchildren that we can be proud of.

Our nation was founded on the principles of justice and equality, but we know that these principles have not always been fully realized. Too many Americans have been denied justice and equality because of the color of their skin, their gender, their sexual orientation, or their economic status. This must change, and it must change now.

As your president, I am committed to advancing justice and equality for all Americans. We will work to reform our criminal justice system, addressing the systemic racism that has led to mass incarceration and unequal treatment under the law. We will invest in community-based alternatives to incarceration, end the use of private prisons, and ensure that every person is treated with dignity and respect.

We will also protect and expand voting rights, ensuring that every American has the right to vote and that every vote is counted. We will pass comprehensive voting rights legislation that ends voter suppression, restores the Voting Rights Act, and makes it easier for every American to participate in our democracy.

We will advance civil rights by protecting LGBTQ+ rights, ensuring equal pay for equal work, and addressing discrimination in all its forms. We will work to end gender-based violence, protect reproductive rights, and ensure that every person has the right to make decisions about their own body.

But justice and equality are not just about laws and policies; they are about changing hearts and minds. We must work together to build a society that values every person, regardless of their race, gender, or background. We must confront the legacy of racism and discrimination in our country and work to create a more just and inclusive society.

As we address the challenges here at home, we must also recognize that we live in an interconnected world. The challenges we face—whether it is climate change, global pandemics, or economic inequality—do not stop at our borders. We must work with our international partners to address these challenges and to build a more peaceful and just world.

As your president, I am committed to restoring American leadership on the global stage. We will re-engage with our allies, rebuild our relationships, and strengthen our alliances. We will work with our partners to address global challenges, from climate change to terrorism, and to promote human rights and democracy around the world.

We will also prioritize diplomacy as the primary tool of our foreign policy. We will work to resolve conflicts through negotiation and dialogue, rather than through force. We will support peacekeeping missions, humanitarian efforts, and international institutions that promote peace and security.

But global leadership is not just about power; it is about values. We must lead by example, showing the world that we are committed to justice, equality, and human rights. We must use our influence to promote these values around the world and to support those who are fighting for freedom and democracy.

As I stand before you today, I am filled with hope for the future of our country. I believe in the strength of the American people, in our resilience, our creativity, and our capacity for progress. I believe that we can overcome the challenges we face and build a future that is fairer, more just, and more inclusive.

But I also know that this will not be easy. The road ahead will be difficult, and there will be times when we are tested. But I have faith in the American people, and I have faith in our democracy. I believe that together, we can build a future that reflects our highest ideals and our deepest values.

Today, I ask for your help in this endeavor. I ask for your partnership, your commitment, and your determination. Together, we can make our country stronger, our economy more just, our healthcare system more accessible, our planet more sustainable, and our society more equitable.

Let us remember that we are all in this together, that we are stronger when we stand united, and that our best days are still ahead of us. Let us work together to build a future that we can be proud of, a future that reflects the values of justice, equality, and opportunity for all.

Thank you, and may God bless you, and may God bless the
United States of America.

Don't miss out!

Visit the website below and you can sign up to receive emails whenever Vivian Ellis publishes a new book. There's no charge and no obligation.

https://books2read.com/r/B-A-ZWVEC-ZDGNE

BOOKS 2 READ

Connecting independent readers to independent writers.